Patterns for e-business

A Strategy for Reuse

"This is one of the most practically useful books on IT there is. I can recommend it to executives of companies that depend on IT for their competitive edge, particularly those where e-business is part of their operation or their future plans. And I can recommend it to every level of IT professional—from the CIO down to the programmer. It is about how to build large computer systems that will work and is written by experts in the field. Not only will it educate, but it provides free access to a wealth of experience—in its pages and also in the remarkably well-organized Web site that backs it up. If your job involves IT systems, then I suggest you read it."

Robin Bloor
CEO
Bloor Research
www.bloor-research.com

"The innovative business processes required by e-business demand systems architectures that are truly integrated and can evolve with the enterprise. This book provides practical insight, derived from hundreds of customer experiences, on how Patterns for e-business can be used to help companies speed up their development process and enable business strategies with high-quality systems solutions."

Frank Roney
General Manager, Worldwide Business Innovation Services
IBM Global Services

"These are early days for e-business and it seems likely that the ability to handle complexity, and deliver systems in a timely manner, will ultimately become business critical factors; the 'Patterns for e-business' initiative is a frontal assault on proliferating complexity and shrinking windows of opportunity, and management should at least investigate the potential it offers for their own business."

Martin Butler
Chairman
Butler Group
www.butlergroup.com

Patterns for e-business

A Strategy for Reuse

**Jonathan Adams, Srinivas Koushik,
Guru Vasudeva, and George Galambos**

Patterns for e-business: A Strategy for Reuse
Jonathan Adams, Srinivas Koushik, Guru Vasudeva, and George Galambos

Published by IBM Press™
Program Director, IBM Centre for Advanced Studies (CAS): Gabriel Silberman
IBM Associate Publisher: Joe Wigglesworth
IBM Press Alliance Publisher: David Uptmor, MC Press, LLC
Developmental Editor: Jill Batistick

For information on translations or book distribution outside the United States or to arrange
bulk-purchase discounts for sales promotions or premiums please contact:

IBM Press
c/o MC Press, LLC
125 N. Woodland Trail
Double Oak, TX 75077
USA
817-961-0660 (corporate offices)
877-226-5394 (sales and customer service)
www.mcpressonline.com/ibmpress

First edition
First printing: October 2001
Second printing: February 2002

ISBN: 1-931182-02-7

To my wife, Barbara, and my sons, Richard and David
J.A.

To my dad, Dr. Veeraraghavan
S.K.

To my wife Rashmi Nemade
G.V.

To my wife, Aniko, and my children, Jill and Johnny
G.G.

Acknowledgments

The original Patterns for e-business, which were published on the "Patterns for e-business" Web site prior to September 2001, had many respected IBM contributors. Key among these were Dr. Barry Devlin, Joel Farrell, Leo Marland, Ian McCallion, John Medicke, John Rothwell, Carla Sadtler and the rest of the ITSO Redbook team, along with the authors of this book.

We are indebted to these architects and their many colleagues who helped to build the bedrock of the Patterns for e-business on which this book was built. We would also like to recognize Pete Smith and Stacey Miller, who have worked tirelessly with Jonathan Adams to organize, cajole, publish, and communicate the Patterns for e-business message inside and outside IBM.

In particular, we would like to thank John Vlissides for a very perceptive review of an early draft that led to significant structural rework and, we hope, a more approachable book. Other IBM architects have also provided valuable reviews of individual chapters.

Three of the four authors of this book are practicing software architects working on real customer engagements. We make no apologies for applying the test of pragmatism rather than purity when hard decisions have had to be made. That, after all, is the choice any practicing architect or engineer would make!

Jonathan Adams, *jonathan_adams@uk.ibm.com*
Srinivas Koushik, *skoushik@us.ibm.com*
Guru Vasudeva, *vasudeva@us.ibm.com*
George Galambos, *galambos@ca.ibm.com*

Contents

Foreword

Paul Harmon
founding editor *Component Development Strategies* newsletter

When I first encountered IBM's "Patterns for e-business" Web site, I was both interested and skeptical. I was interested in the idea of extending patterns to a new level of abstraction—to business process design—and worried that these patterns might not be derived from actual experience. As I've investigated, however, I've been satisfied that the IBM researchers are truly working in the best tradition of the patterns movement. These are not arbitrary solutions proposed by theorists. Instead, IBM has taken advantage of its large, worldwide consulting practice to gather information about successful solutions that customers have actually implemented. Of course, when one works at a higher level of abstraction, defining boundaries is always difficult. Patterns, after all, are only useful if a potential user can find one that describes a solution to the specific problem the user faces.

In this book, Adams, Koushik, Vasudeva, and Galambos have stepped back from the specific Patterns for e-business that IBM has documented, and developed a conceptual framework that business analysts can use when they seek to define the problems they face. Then, they can determine which of the various patterns will best serve their needs.

Unfortunately for the business analyst, the Internet has the power to improve so many different aspects of the modern enterprise that e-business applications often seem to involve changes in every different group and application in the company. It's not uncommon to find companies creating Web portals that let users examine options and then tailor products. As soon as a user has tailored a product and agreed to buy it, related systems proceed to arrange credit for the buyer, order the parts required from suppliers, and schedule and arrange to ship the resulting product to the new customer. To deal with this kind of scope and complexity, the authors have created a way of classifying the different types of Patterns for e-business. They begin by first identifying six core patterns, and then describe how these patterns can be combined to create more complex systems.

Again, because of the complexity and the level of abstraction involved, the authors have not been content to simply define a single high-level set of patterns for e-business and discuss their various combinations. Realizing that a company may seek to implement an early e-business application and then progressively enhance it, the authors have defined high-level business patterns and then defined a number of application patterns that could be used to implement each business pattern. Thus, once a business team decides that it should use a business-to-business pattern, it can consider several different business-to-business application patterns, ranging from the simple to the very complex, to implement the business-to-business pattern. Moreover, once the e-business team has identified a business pattern and an application pattern, IBM provides, on its Web site, a number of specific implementation patterns that incorporate constraints imposed by specific hardware and operating-system choices.

The authors enable analysts to combine the Patterns for e-business and arrange the patterns in hierarchies. This allows analysts to start at an abstract level and drill down to more specific patterns. These are major contributions in the use of patterns.

More important than any theoretical contributions to the pattern movements, however, are the practical values of this book. Figuring out how to use the Internet to more successfully serve customers and to increase the efficiency of internal business processes will be among the dominant business goals of this decade. Indeed, companies that do not manage to make effective use of the Internet and related technologies are unlikely to survive to 2010. Most business managers know this, and they are eager to figure out how their companies can transition to e-business. The problem, however, is that the popular press is filled with stories about all of the different ways companies have used the Internet. Each article uses slightly different terms to describe what was done. Dozens of vendors offer different products, each designed to solve a single part of the overall e-business problem. It's easy to get overwhelmed by a seemingly immense number of options. That's where this book comes in.

I don't know of any book that will provide business managers with a better overview of the practical options they face as they consider an e-business transition. It considers ways each of the options can be combined with others to create even more comprehensive strategies. It also provides enough detail so that the more technically inclined manager can drill down and see what would be involved in actually implementing any one of these e-business processes. Importantly, these options aren't just the figments of some designer's imagination; they are solutions that have already been tried, and which have succeeded at other companies like yours. These are patterns with a proven track record.

The Patterns for e-business provide an ideal way to communicate options and best practices. This book lets a manager know about the patterns that major companies are employing as they seek to improve their business processes for the coming decade. If you are trying to figure out what your company can do to make the best use of the Internet, this is the place to start.

Foreword

John Vlissides
IBM T.J. Watson Research

Ever wonder what happens when you press the "Place Your Order" button on your favorite e-commerce site—especially when it takes an eternity to get a response? A whole lot of cycles are being spent somewhere. Some of the delay is explained by network latency, but not all, or the response would be much more erratic than it is.

Truth be told, there's a huge amount of processing going on behind the scenes. The browser talks to the server, the server to the middleware, the middleware to one or more databases, the databases to other databases, and all the way back. Objects are created and destroyed again and again, often hundreds of times per transaction. Connections are made, broken, and remade. Layer upon layer of software is traversed by any number of threads. It's all so big and complex, it's a wonder it works at all. And yet it works well enough that untold millions of e-business transactions take place around the Internet every day.

Unfortunately, making good on the "e-business" appellation remains a black art. The tragedy is that it needn't be so, despite the complexity. Few businesses require truly novel online solutions. Much of the effort involved in deploying an e-business is pure reinvention. That's not to say every business is the same; far from it. But the set of fundamental problems businesses face is quite finite. What's crucial are the abstractions into which to distill the commonalities.

And not just any abstractions. Consider the periodic table of the elements. Imagine how hard it was to reason about matter before Mendeleev had that bright idea. He wasn't the first to dream up an abstraction along these lines. It's just that earlier abstractions, such as the Greeks' water-air-earth-fire paradigm, came up short after a while. They hit the brick wall of reality, as it were, after which they proved useless. The key difference was that Mendeleev's abstraction was far better grounded in reality. It never encountered such a wall—not yet, at least.

So, reality is key, as are the right abstractions. How do you communicate them? My co-authors and I (see Gamma et al., 1995 in the Bibliography) have long held that the pattern form could be used to disseminate any expertise, not just town, building, and (software) construction. But I, for one, was convinced it would be a long time before there were patterns for something as new and sprawling as e-business. It would take years, maybe decades, before all the ingredients could converge:

- Stable, reasonably well-understood e-business requirements

- A critical mass of experience building e-business applications

- A set of authors with the time, energy, ability, and drive to do the hard work of unearthing the patterns, characterizing them, and writing them up in lucid and potent form

The concept of e-business is fairly old hat by now; the second and third items are the interesting ones. Who could have the right conditions to make them happen? The answer, as it turned out, lay very close to home: IBM Global Services (IGS). It's an organization with few peers in sheer size and scope of projects, to say nothing of its members' talents. (And I say that advisedly, given my affiliation and all.) What's more, IGS had something no one else could boast in the persons of Adams,

Koushik, Vasudeva, and Galambos—a crack team with combined experience in e-business engagements measured in decades.

Which brings me to the book you're holding now. These authors have produced a work with the distinction of being both first and foremost in the abstractions it offers. That it's first is a matter of public record: I know of no earlier work along these lines. That the patterns are effective is self-evident, as they were mined from a wide array of real e-business systems and the engagements that produced them.

The authors' decomposition of the commonalities is perhaps their greatest contribution. But that's just the half of it. These guys have put legs to the right abstractions by including hard-won experience, specifically in the form of succinct characterizations of recurring e-business problems and their attendant solutions, complete with discussions of trade-offs, benefits, and liabilities—the stuff of patterns worthy of the name.

It doesn't matter whether you're a large multinational corporation, a sole proprietorship, or something in between. The patterns in this book will give you the wherewithal to put your business online with a minimum of reinvention, expense, blood, sweat, and tears. Prepare to experience the benefits that other pattern communities have enjoyed since well before the dawn of e-business.

About this book

This book should be of interest to all those who wish to understand how to reuse the e-business architectures successfully employed by many innovative organizations in the growing digital economy. It is targeted to a wide audience, including the following:

- **Business executives** who make decisions on the e-business solutions that are implemented within their organization and are conscious of the key drivers (such as time to market and cost to implement) that govern the implementation of these solutions

- **Chief information officers (CIOs) and chief technology officers (CTOs)** who are responsible for implementing the e-business solutions and making decisions on the architecture that will provide the underpinnings of these solutions.

- **Technical professionals**, including independent software vendors (ISVs), Web integrators, system integrators, and solution architects, who need to be able to translate complex business requirements into applications that can be implemented using a specific set of technologies.

- The **academic community** who wish to understand the approaches used by practitioners in implementing e-business solutions.

If you are a business executive, you might find it sufficient to first read Chapters 1 through 6, and next read Chapter 13, leaving out the running case study in these chapters. Then, read the first half of Chapter 14, which provides a case study applying the techniques in the earlier chapters.

If you are a technical executive, you are encouraged to read Chapters 1 through 6, including the running case study, plus the introductory pages to the Application patterns in Chapters 7 through 12. Follow this by reading all of Chapters 13 and 14 for a good understanding of how to assemble complex solutions using the Patterns for e-business.

If you are a technical reader, you will probably need to read the whole book, although you can read Chapters 7 through 10 in any preferred order. It might be helpful to start with the Application pattern chapter closest to your business domain knowledge. This will enable you to comfortably acquire an understanding of the style and semantics of the Application pattern descriptions before looking at less familiar patterns. The IT architect should then embark on a review of other relevant patterns, using the CD-ROM packaged with this book, the "Patterns for e-business" Web site at http://www.ibm.com/framework/patterns, and the relevant Redbooks at http://www.ibm.com/developerworks/patterns/library/index.html.

Chapter summaries

Chapter 1 reviews the key characteristics of the digital economy and then discusses the range of business solutions that can be developed to fully exploit this new economy.

Chapter 2 introduces the concept of the Patterns for e-business and positions them with respect to the design and architecture patterns prevalent in the field of software engineering. The four types of Patterns for e-business (Business, Integration, Application, and Runtime patterns) are described, with this book deliberately limited to covering Business, Integration, and Application patterns. The iconic representation of these patterns is introduced as used throughout the book. Finally, the first case study is described. This case study is used as a running example to illustrate the techniques described in later chapters.

Chapter 3 describes a common framework for documenting the Patterns for e-business. This framework provides consistency and improves readability. It is consistent with the structure and approach used by earlier work in this field.

Chapter 4 describes the Business patterns that represent the highest level of abstraction. Out of all the possible Business patterns, the four primary ones are identified:

- Self-Service

- Collaboration

- Information Aggregation

- Extended Enterprise

These primary Business patterns provide the building blocks for composing most e-business solutions.

Chapter 5 discusses Integration patterns. These patterns serve two purposes. First, they are used to combine Business patterns to enable more advanced e-business solutions. (The combining is actually done at the Application pattern level for each Business pattern.) Second, they can be used within a Business pattern to integrate core business applications and databases. (Again, this integration is done at the Application pattern level for a particular Business pattern.) Two types of Integration patterns are described:

- Access Integration

- Application Integration

Chapter 6 introduces the concept of combining a number of Business and Integration patterns to implement an installation-specific solution. We call this combination of patterns a *custom design*. The chapter then describes the harvesting of commonly occurring combinations of Business and Integration patterns to make Composite patterns.

Chapters 7 through 12 describe the Application patterns that can be used to automate the Business and Integration patterns described in the earlier chapters.

Chapter 13 draws together the conclusion of the analysis and documents the next steps that a customer IT architect or system integrator needs to take.

Chapter 14 provides a second case study based on a detailed e-Marketplace example to illustrate the use of the patterns and techniques identified in this book. The example is based on a real-life engagement, with some key details changed to make it more comprehensive.

Patterns capitalization scheme

When one of the Patterns for e-business is referenced in the text, the following capitalization scheme is used:

- *Business pattern*
- *Self-Service business pattern*
- *Collaboration business pattern*
- *Information Aggregation business pattern*
- *Extended Enterprise business pattern*
- *Integration pattern*
- *Access Integration pattern* (Although slightly inconsistent, keeping *Integration* capitalized keeps the correct focus on integration.)
- *Application Integration pattern*
- *Composite pattern*, or for a specific Composite pattern, *Electronic Commerce composite pattern*
- *Application pattern*, or for a specific Application pattern, *Router application pattern*
- *Runtime pattern*

Solutions
for a digital economy

The Internet has been growing rapidly, with more and more users across the globe going online every day. While just a few years ago the Internet was used primarily by academic institutions and the military, in today's economy, millions of people use the Internet to buy goods and services, manage their financial portfolios, collaborate with others, and check the latest news. In a very short time, the Internet has become an indispensable tool that is used in every facet of our daily lives. The pervasive nature of the Internet and its growing numbers of users make the Internet and its underlying technologies a top priority for organizations that plan to lead and dominate in their respective industries.

Competing in the digital economy

As Internet technologies continue to mature and become engrained in our daily lives, a new phenomenon is starting to emerge: applications, systems, and even enterprises are no longer islands, but are parts of an overall ecosystem where, much like in nature, they exist through complex and ever-changing dynamic relationships with one another. An organization that succeeds in this environment will:

- Have a sustainable business model that provides profitable returns and a dependable revenue stream within a reasonable time frame.

- Extend the reach of the enterprise beyond organizational and geographic boundaries and allow the organization to exploit local and global markets.

- Compete aggressively with local and global competitors. The organization should also be flexible and nimble, so it can adapt to an environment where the basis of business competition shifts from cost and value to "imagination." Success in such an environment is determined by the speed at which new creative ideas are generated, synthesized, and then implemented with entrepreneurial zeal and dynamism.

- Focus on attracting and retaining a large and sustainable set of customers by providing them with compelling value, personalized service, and around-the-clock access to products and services.

- Strive for efficiency by optimizing all the links in its value chain. In his groundbreaking work in 1980, Michael Porter described the value chain as the set of activities an organization performs to create and distribute its goods and services[1]. These services include direct activities (such as procurement and production) and indirect activities (such as human resource management and financial management). Each of these activities adds value to the product. Increasing the effectiveness of the value chain increases the competitiveness of the organization. To reinvent the value chain, an organization must rethink its core business processes, which include, but are not limited to, the following:

  - Buying products and services required for its core business processes.

  - Selling its finished products or services to its customers and partners.

  - Sharing and communicating information across the links in the value chain, both within the organization and with its customers and suppliers.

  - Optimizing its supply chain by addressing the inherent inefficiencies in inter-department and inter-enterprise interactions.

  - Designing and launching new products.

  - Exploring new and emerging channels into the marketplace.

- Rapidly sense and respond to changing market conditions. This is what Stephan Haeckel refers to as a sense-and-respond organization. In his 1999 book, *The Adaptive Enterprise*[2], he defines a sense-and-respond organization as one that does not attempt to predict future demand for its offerings. Instead, it identifies changing customer needs and new business challenges as they happen, responds to them quickly and appropriately, and does so before these new opportunities disappear or change into something else

- Be a thought leader by leveraging industry knowledge and market position to provide value-added services to their value chain partners.

Competing based on these objectives in the digital economy demands the development and deployment of some key e-business solutions.

e-business solutions

e-business solutions are not just about technology. They use evolutionary technology and re-engineered business processes to develop revolutionary new applications that are not limited by time, space, organizational boundaries, or territorial borders. This combination of technology and processes supports the emerging set of business priorities, which include greater speed to market, more flexibility and nimbleness, accelerated global expansion, and tighter supplier and customer integration. In this model, networks must support interactivity and transport rich content, helping customers and businesses redefine concepts such as value, competitiveness, and the very nature of transactions. These solutions affect all areas of an organization and fundamentally change how organizations:

- Buy and sell products

- Collaborate within the organization and with their customers, suppliers, and vendors

- Manage their supply chains

- Design and launch products

To succeed in today's digital economy, organizations should transform themselves into e-businesses. They can do this by developing a comprehensive and visionary business strategy grounded in the practical and effective use of Internet technologies. This strategy can then be implemented rapidly and incrementally in the form of leading-edge e-business solutions.

Our definition of e-business solutions includes all applications that allow an enterprise to leverage Internet technologies to re-engineer business processes; enhance communications; and lower organizational barriers with customers and shareholders (across the Internet), employees and stakeholders (across the corporate intranet), and vendors, suppliers and partners (across the corporate extranet). This comprehensive definition of e-business solutions is represented in Figure 1.1.

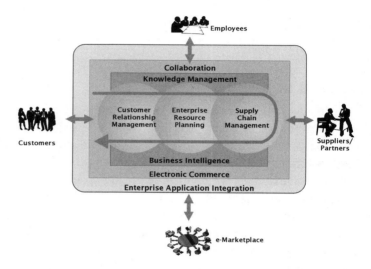

Figure 1.1: There are many user and e-business solution dependencies both within and outside the organization.

Customer relationship management

Customer Relationship Management (CRM) is the essential business process that encompasses an organization's end-to-end engagement with its customers over the lifetime of its relationship with them. CRM sub-processes include prospecting, marketing, sales, customer service, and support. These sub-processes cover all the ways in which customers and the business can interact (person to person, store, branch, call center, kiosk, voice-response unit, ATM, and the Internet).

Enterprise resource planning

Enterprise Resource Planning (ERP) provides the major back-office applications for many enterprises. The most frequently cited benefits of ERP center around process automation and integration, and the availability of data to support business analysis. ERP often requires the top-to-bottom transformation of the way a company operates, does business, and plans for the future.

Supply-chain management

Supply-chain management refers to a set of solutions that allows an enterprise to tie together the people and processes—both internal and external—associated with its flow of goods. Successful supply-chain management allows an enterprise to anticipate demand and deliver the right product to the right place at the right time, at the lowest possible cost, to satisfy its customers. These solutions aim to improve the efficiency of all the links in the value chain by providing measurable benefits to the business such as reduced costs, faster cycle times, and improved product quality.

Electronic commerce

Electronic commerce solutions allow enterprises to offer products and services to existing and new customers across new channels based on Internet technologies. They also provide the foundation for managing electronic transactions and allow customers to browse for and purchase goods and services with convenience and confidence, knowing that their transactions are secure and their privacy is protected.

Business intelligence

Business intelligence is the discipline of developing solutions that are conclusive, fact-based, and actionable. These solutions help the enterprises combine and analyze disparate data sources and derive valuable information from this data that provides key insights and data points that can be used to make informed and intelligent business decisions. These solutions typically include techniques such as data warehousing, data mining, trend analysis and executive information systems.

Knowledge management

Knowledge management is the identification and analysis of available and required knowledge assets and related processes. It also includes the subsequent planning and control of actions to develop both the assets and the processes to fulfill organizational objectives. Knowledge assets are comprised of the knowledge regarding markets, products, technologies, and organizations that a business owns or needs to own and that enable its business processes to generate profits and provide value.

e-Marketplaces

e-Marketplaces are trading exchanges that facilitate and promote buying and selling, and enable business communities among trading partners within certain industries. In these marketplaces, a market maker seeks to control the point of commerce by creating marketplace liquidity and providing a value-added trading alternative to buyers and sellers.

There are two types of marketplaces. *Vertical markets* deal with specialized goods and services used by a specific industry or segment. For example, a vertical marketplace for computer manufacturers might cover printed circuit boards, memory chips, and other integrated circuit chips. *Horizontal markets* address expenditures that are applicable across a wide range of industries, such as office supplies, business services, or temporary employees.

Collaboration

Doing business is a series of collaborative processes. It requires interaction among employees, vendors, suppliers, and business partners. Although e-mail is one example of an indispensable communication tool used by companies around the world, a number of other collaborative applications are increasingly coming into play. These solutions enable local work groups, or even geographically dispersed teams, to work together using real-time information sharing and distribution across the Internet. In addition to e-mail, these solutions include instant messaging, group calendaring and scheduling, shared document libraries, discussion databases, and newsgroups.

Enterprise application integration

Integration and interoperability are critical for realizing the true potential of e-business solutions. Most "brick-and-mortar" enterprises have significant investments in legacy systems and ERP solutions. Thus, to be effective, it is important to integrate these e-business solutions with the ERP systems, legacy applications, and databases that might exist within the organization. It is also important to make sure that these solutions can integrate and interoperate with similar solutions that might exist in other organizations in the value chain.

Implementing e-business solutions

e-business applications are different from the traditional client/server applications developed in the past decade. Table 1.1 illustrates the differences between these two applications.

Table 1.1: *Moving from traditional client/server applications to e-business applications*

	Traditional client/server applications	e-business applications
Reach	Within a department or enterprise	Across departments, enterprises, and geographic and national borders
Architecture	Deployed using a two- or three-tier architecture	Deployed using a thin client architecture with one to N back-end tiers
Programming model	Event-driven, with the application state managed at each client desktop	Thin browser-based clients, with the application state managed in the server layer
Network	LAN- or WAN-based	Based on LANs, WANs, private virtual networks, and Internet connections
Standards	Typically proprietary technologies	Open technologies
Number of users	Predictable user loads, from tens to hundreds	Unpredictable user loads, with massive swings in the number of users

The structure and nature of e-business solutions pose certain challenges to organizations that implement these solutions:

- *A higher degree of integration.* e-business solutions typically implement radically new business processes in support of new and emerging business models, but these solutions need to integrate and work with other systems in the enterprise, including legacy systems and databases. This challenge is magnified in B2B e-business solutions, where the business processes and integration extend across enterprises.

- *The need for speed.* These solutions typically have a very short window for implementation. This urgency increases the risk of these solutions in the areas of technology, architecture, systems testing, and overall project management. This appears to conflict with the conventional wisdom of reducing the overall risk of implementation, However, the patterns identified in this book should help mitigate this risk and provide a proven and consistent approach for designing these solutions. This approach is built on the knowledge of experts (captured in these patterns) and promotes the development and reuse of assets based on these patterns.

- *Quality*. These solutions are designed to reach users beyond the enterprise, so it is extremely important to ensure the overall quality of the solution. The overall quality can be measured using quantifiable operational characteristics such as performance, scalability, security, reliability, and availability.

- *The shortage of skills*. These complex solutions require considerable skills to develop and implement. The extremely competitive labor market combined with a genuine shortage of experienced e-business architects and developers creates problems for organizations planning to implement e-business solutions.

- *Changing technology*. The Internet and its technologies are evolving rapidly, causing many interesting problems for enterprises trying to implement e-business solutions. To succeed, these organizations should take stock of how they implement solutions based on these technologies, and build a plan to manage constant changes to the underlying technologies that support their applications.

Many hardware and software vendors in today's marketplace claim to have strategies and approaches that will help guide companies in their transition from an industrial economy to the digital economy. However, a closer look at many of these approaches shows that they are no more than a narrowly focused set of products thrown together to form a roadmap leading to the implementation of certain technologies. A truly powerful and viable strategy should be comprehensive and driven by all the facets of the business, supported effectively by technology. Such a strategy needs to effectively address the challenges identified earlier in this chapter.

The Patterns for e-business described in this book facilitate the implementation of an organization's e-business strategy by relying on proven and reusable architectures and designs. The expert knowledge captured in these patterns also helps mitigate many of the risks associated with the lack of key skills. Finally, since the Patterns for e-business are based on proven designs and cover a wide range of issues, from the business level to technical implementation, they can speed the time to market of many of these solutions.

References

[1]   Porter, Michael.1980. Competitive Strategy. New York: Free Press.

[2]   Haeckel, Stephan H. and Adrian J. Slywotzky. 1999. Adaptive Enterprise: Creating and Leading Sense-and-Respond Organizations. Boston: Harvard Business School Press.

CHAPTER 2

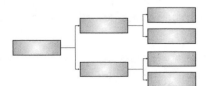

Patterns for e-business

The concept of patterns is not new; they have been used extensively in the fields of design and architecture for centuries. In fact, some of the most referenced works in the field of patterns are not from software engineers or technologists but from the acclaimed architect, Dr. Christopher Alexander. Dr. Alexander's work and writings have had a significant impact in the area of software solutions. The constructs, ideas, and techniques identified and documented in his writings have been applied extensively to the fields of software engineering and object-oriented programming.

In his 1977 book, *A Pattern Language* [1], Dr. C. Alexander provides a simple and concise description of patterns as they apply to the problems in creating cities and towns, neighborhoods, and buildings:

> Each pattern describes a problem that occurs over and over again in our environment and then describes the core of the solution to that problem in such a way that you can use this solution a million times over without ever doing it the same way twice.

Experienced software engineers will readily accept the fact that the process of developing software has many similarities to the process of developing cities, towns, and buildings. Thus, it is not surprising that the idea of patterns has gained acceptance among software designers and developers. It enables efficiency in both the communication and the implementation of software design, based upon a common vocabulary and reference.

The process of developing patterns in any domain takes experience—lots of it. Over the past six years, IBM has played a significant role in developing the Internet marketplace by providing the technical leadership needed to define and put structure around this rapidly evolving field. IBM has Internet-enabled its product portfolio and has helped its customers implement e-business applications. This application base spans all major industries, and ranges from static Web sites to some of the most complex transaction-processing applications on the Web today. Some of the most commonly occurring patterns are described in this book.

It is important to remember that patterns are not just concepts, but practical and actionable constructs derived from experience in building real-life applications. Patterns help capture and codify expert knowledge and make it possible to share that knowledge with others. In general, patterns are not invented, but are identified and mined from extensive experience in a particular field. Patterns enable you to rapidly develop solutions without sacrificing the quality and service expected from those solutions. They also make sure that the knowledge gained from the implementation of solutions is shared, to avoid reinventing answers to problems that have already been solved.

Patterns in software development

In the context of developing software applications, the architecture of the solution should address two major domains: the *functional domain* and the *operational domain*. The functional domain addresses the business functionality of the solution, the structure and modularity of the software components that will be used to implement the business functions, the interactions between the components, and the interfaces between them. The operational domain describes the system organization (such as hardware platforms, connections, locations, and topology), the placement of software and data components, the service requirements (such as performance, availability, and security), and the system management (capacity planning, software distribution, backup, and recovery).

There is clear evidence of patterns in both of these domains. *System-level patterns* identify and describe the overall structure and interactions that can occur between components of a system. These patterns can typically be used during the high-level design phase to develop the structure of the overall application solution. The authors of *Pattern-Oriented Software Architecture—A System of Patterns* [2] identified patterns for system architecture at a higher level than the original design patterns. Their patterns relate to the macro-design of system components such as operating systems or network stacks.

Design patterns represent the original, and currently most comprehensive, description of more granular patterns that can aid the design of software components. In their ground-breaking book, *Design Patterns: Elements of Reusable Object-Oriented Software* [3], the authors, often referred to as the "Gang of Four," document 23 patterns recognized as providing accepted solutions for recurring problems in object-oriented design. These patterns help software designers establish the structure and operation of the code that supports the functional components of the application.

These patterns have focused primarily on the design and programming phases of application development, dealing with the structure and behavior of the code that supports the application.

Introducing the Patterns for e-business

Chapter 1 introduces e-business solutions, showing how these solutions span multiple business domains and are more complex to implement than traditional application systems. These solutions require a constant and clear exchange of ideas and information between the business owners driving the solution and the IT personnel responsible for its implementation. While constructs such as design patterns are still very useful in the development of the solution, they have minimal impact in the early stages of the solution design, where key decisions are made regarding the solution's overall structure and end-to-end architecture.

The Patterns for e-business introduced in this book extend the domain of software patterns to earlier phases of the application development life cycle. These patterns help us understand and analyze complex business problems and break them down into smaller, more manageable functions that can then be implemented using lower-level design patterns. There are four major types of Patterns for e-business:

- Business
- Integration
- Application
- Runtime

The Business and Integration patterns have the same structure, as shown in Figure 2.1.

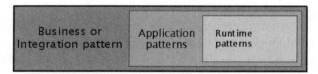

Figure 2.1: Business and Integration patterns have the same structure.

Business patterns

Business patterns are high-level constructs used to establish the primary business purpose of any solution. These patterns help establish three key aspects of any solution:

- They define the major objectives of the solution. For instance, a Self-Service business pattern is observed in solutions that enable users to access systems directly, without going through a service intermediary (such as an insurance agent or a customer-service representative).

- They identify the high-level participants who interact in the solution.

- They help us understand and describe the nature of the interactions that occur between the participants.

It is important to note that the concept of Business patterns transcends the domain of computers and systems. In other words, the Business patterns identified in this book can be observed in any solution you interact with on a daily basis. For instance, the Collaboration business pattern can be observed in daily business operations such as conference calls, sending and receiving voice mail, and participating in face-to-face meetings.

Integration patterns

Integration patterns help to implement a full solution, integrating the individual Business patterns to satisfy the full e-business requirements. The integration is actually done at the Application pattern level for each Business pattern. Integration patterns can also be used within a Business pattern to integrate core business applications and databases. These patterns implement the specific interactions between the logical components that make up the Application pattern. Again, this integration is done at the Application pattern level for the Business pattern.

Overall, Integration patterns help provide:

- A seamless customer experience to the users of the solution. These patterns provide a single sign-on function to multiple back-end systems, personalized user interfaces, and the ability to support the same customer experience across multiple devices.

- Varying levels of integration with the applications and databases that exist within the organization.

Application patterns

Application patterns help refine Business patterns so that they can be implemented as computer-based solutions. These patterns help provide structure to the Business patterns by identifying and describing the high-level logical components needed to implement the key functions of each Business pattern. Specifically, Application patterns represent the partitioning of the application logic and data together with the styles of interaction between the logic tiers. Application patterns serve as the foundation for the subsequent critical step: the placement of the application and data elements on top of the middleware structure.

Usually, more than one Application pattern can be used to automate a Business pattern. Which Application pattern to use depends on the key business and IT drivers unique to the organization. For instance, when implementing the Self-Service business pattern as part of a customer site, the choice of Application pattern can be affected by the need to:

- Reduce the latency of business events

- Provide a unified customer view across lines of business (LOB)

- Enable easy adaptation during mergers and acquisitions

A different combination of these business drivers might lead to the selection of a different Application pattern.

Runtime patterns

Runtime patterns are used to define the logical middleware structure supporting the Application pattern. In other words, Runtime patterns describe the logical architecture required to implement an Application pattern. Runtime patterns depict the major middleware nodes, their roles, and the interfaces between these nodes. These patterns also address how the processing logic and data are placed on these nodes. Like Application patterns, Runtime patterns represent logical constructs put together in a predefined structure that enables the solution to provide acceptable service levels to its users. The logical nodes can then be translated into a physical implementation, using vendor product mappings, recommended best practices, and personal experience. The technologies used for the physical implementation will be varied—and include the use of Web services. More details on this emerging technology and related Runtime patterns can be found on the Patterns for e-business Website (http://www.ibm.com/framework/patterns).

More than one Runtime pattern might work for a particular Application pattern, as shown in Figure 2.2. The process of selecting the appropriate alternative involves evaluating the specific operational requirements (such as security, scalability, and ease of maintenance) that might apply to the solution.

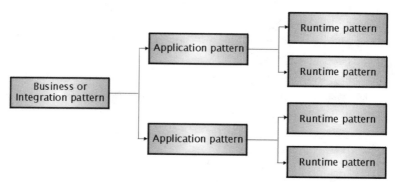

Figure 2.2: For each Business or Integration pattern, there can be more than one Application pattern. For each Application pattern, there can be more than one Runtime pattern.

Applying the Patterns for e-business

The combination of Business/Integration, Application, and Runtime patterns provides a clear and consistent approach to bridge the divide that sometimes arises between the business and IT departments within an organization. The Patterns for e-business are also relevant to a wider spectrum of users:

- Line-of-business executives who understand the business aspects and requirements of the solution can use Business patterns to develop a high-level structure for the solution.

- Senior technical executives can work with the line-of-business executives to agree on the structure of the solution. They can then use the Application patterns to make critical decisions related to the structure of the solution, as well as the architectural decisions needed to implement the solution.

- Solution architects and systems designers can work with the business and technical executives to arrive at the solution structure and the key architectural decisions. They can then develop a technical architecture by using Runtime patterns to realize the Application patterns.

Scope of this book

As shown in Figure 2.3, this book provides a detailed overview of Business, Integration, and Application patterns. Runtime patterns are more technical, and require detailed technical discussions that go beyond the scope of this book. For detailed descriptions of Runtime patterns, see the official Web site (http://www.ibm.com/ framework/patterns) and the patterns resources page, which includes the patterns Redbooks (http://www.ibm.com/developerworks/patterns/library/index.html). (Redbooks are technical publications from IBM's International Technical Support Organization, or ITSO.)

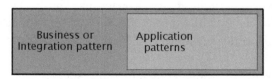

Figure 2.3: The scope of this book is Business, Integration, and Application patterns.

Philosophy of this book

These Patterns for e-business resources capture best practices that apply at various stages of the application development life cycle. Reusing these architectural and design best practices can minimize the overall risk of your projects. Throughout this book, the FutureStep Electronics case study illustrates how you can use the Patterns for e-business resources to reduce both risk and time to market. This is accomplished by means of asset reuse during the early stages of the application development process.

The case study presented in this book applies the following ideas to a concrete problem:

- Most complex e-business problems can be decomposed into simpler problems, each of which can be matched with one of the four primary Business patterns.

- Based on the business and IT drivers, you can choose appropriate Application patterns to automate the Business patterns.

- Integration patterns can be used to combine the chosen Application patterns and compose a complete e-business solution.

- Web-based resources can be used to further elaborate this solution and customize it for your needs.

FutureStep Electronics: a case study

This section describes the application development process at FutureStep Electronics and the high-level requirements of the e-business solution. It also describes how senior executives can pictorially show both the solution and the key participants in the solution. Subsequent chapters introduce additional technical and business requirements that help demonstrate the process of developing the architecture for the solution by combining Business patterns. These chapters also describe how this architecture can be refined further by selecting Application patterns and making critical architectural decisions.

This overall structure can then be implemented as a solution by using other resources dedicated to Patterns for e-business (the Web site and the Redbooks). These resources help define the logical architecture by selecting Runtime patterns, and develop a physical architecture by selecting products that can be used to implement the solution.

The case study

FutureStep Electronics, an electronic parts manufacturing company, wishes to use e-business technologies to implement a customer self-service solution that will give its customers comprehensive, around-the-clock service. The solution will provide the following:

- A personalized customer-service experience

- Access to electronic component information

- Opinions and buying advice that enable customers to make improved buying decisions

- An easy-to-use component ordering process

- Access to financing from outside financial institutions

FutureStep would also like to provide access to these business functions across several channels, including Web browsers across the Internet, personal digital assistants (PDAs), and pagers.

We have simplified many areas of the case study by not including key topics that are typically found in similar solutions, such as order inquiry, order cancellation, fulfillment, and reverse logistics. This was done to facilitate the discussion and keep it focused on the concept of the Patterns for e-business.

Step 1: Develop a high-level business description

In the first step of the solution-definition process, the business owner should develop a high-level business description that illustrates the major business functions of the proposed solution. This description can be simply one or two clearly worded paragraphs describing the actors participating in the solution and the high-level interactions between these actors required by the new or modified business functions. The actor entities will not be modified by this solution, but are critical for the completeness of the overall solution. For example, actors can be people, devices, external institutions, packages, applications, and data that may be accessed but not modified.

To better understand this concept, consider the following business description for the FutureStep solution. (The underlined items identify the actors in the solution, and the items in **bold** represent the high-level business functions that need to be provided or modified by the solution.)

The FutureStep Electronics Customer Service (FECS) solution provides an end-to-end customer-service solution for our business customers, who are end-product manufacturers that use our electronic components. The FECS solution should support a browser-based interface (and other widely available device interfaces) and be accessible across the Internet.

The FECS system allows customers to **register** their names, locations, shipping addresses, preferred financial institutions, and other relevant information. This function also allows customers to change passwords, set user interface parameters, and perform other online account-maintenance functions.

Customers can log in to the FECS system and **select** components from a product catalog. They can optionally enter a **product research forum**, where they can learn more about the experiences of other manufacturers, in the form of structured content providing the key design specifications, assembly advice, and reliability and desirable service strategies appropriate for their line of finished products. The information from this forum can also be accessed by customers as a research tool, even when they are not browsing through the catalog. This information comes from FutureStep's internal **knowledge base** or from data available on other related Web sites on the Internet.

When the customer wants to **place an order**, the FECS system verifies that the component is available by querying the in-house inventory control application. It also links to a **financing application** that lets the customer select from several financing options provided by different financial institutions. FECS automatically accesses the customer's preferences and other profile information from the **customer registration** database to complete the details of the order. Once the order is saved, the customer is **notified** electronically via e-mail or pager. The completed order is then forwarded via e-mail to the warehouse to be filled and shipped to the customer.

This short business description captures the high-level requirements of the business problem outlined in this case study.

Step 2: Develop a Solution Overview Diagram

The next step is to develop a Solution Overview Diagram that helps translate the textual description provided by the business description into a pictorial representation. Once again, the objective is to keep the diagram simple and informative. Four major symbols facilitate this:

- A rectangle represents a high-level new or modified business function.

- A rectangle with two vertical lines represents a predefined function, which is an application or package that will interface with the solution, but will not be modified or changed by it. (In other words, it is one of the actors.)

- A picture or other icon represents other actors.

- A connector links the other three symbols.

The Solution Overview Diagram can be drawn in a few simple stages. The first stage is to analyze the business description developed in the previous section and draw rectangles to represent the key business functions (the items in **bold** in the description). For instance, from the business description, you can identify the following functions in the FECS system (the terms in parentheses are used in the description):

- Customer financing (financing application)

- Customer notification (notified electronically)

- Order entry (place an order)

- Customer registration (register)

- Product selection (select)

- Product research forum (product research forum)

- Product knowledge base (knowledge base)

The second stage is to represent any predefined processes (such as the inventory control system) by a rectangle with two vertical lines. The third stage is to use pictures or icons to represent all the remaining actors in the business description. These include the following:

- Customer
- Browser
- PDA
- Pager
- Warehouse
- Financial institutions
- Other (external) Web sites

The result is shown in Figure 2.4.

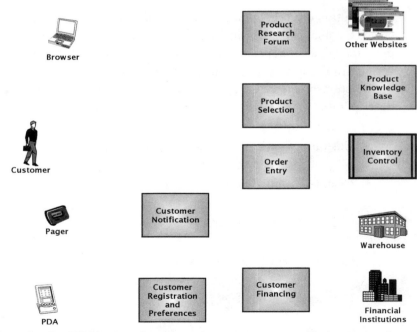

Figure 2.4: The FECS business functions and actors are represented in the process of developing a Solution Overview Diagram.

The last stage is to use the business description to walk through each process and link the individual symbols using connectors. This produces the completed Solution Overview Diagram shown in Figure 2.5.

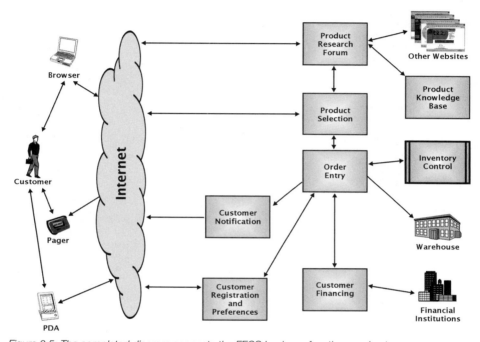

Figure 2.5: The completed diagram connects the FECS business functions and actors.

The Solution Overview Diagram provides a concise and comprehensive way of representing key aspects of the proposed solution. It provides the foundation for the process of identifying and applying the Patterns for e-business. The discussion of this solution and the solution development process continues after the concept of Business patterns is introduced in Chapter 4.

References

[1] Alexander, C., et al. 1977. A Pattern Language. New York: Oxford University Press.

[2] Buschmann, F., Meunier, R., Rohnert, H., Sommerlad, P., and M. Stal. 1996. Pattern-Oriented Software Architecture, A System of Patterns. New York: John Wiley and Sons.

[3]   Gamma, E., Helm, R., Johnson, R., and J. Vlissides. 1995. Design Patterns: Elements of Reusable Object-Oriented Software. Reading, MA: Addison-Wesley.

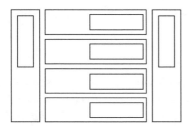

Documenting the Patterns for e-business

This chapter describes the documentation principles used in this book. These include the visual and textual notation used to represent the patterns, and the standard framework used to fully document the patterns.

Visual notation

Chapter 2 introduces the Patterns for e-business and shows how to represent these patterns using a simple diagram. The remaining chapters use the notation in Figure 3.1 to represent the Patterns for e-business. Figure 3.1 builds on the simple notation described in Chapter 2 by showing the existence of multiple Business patterns and two distinct types of Integration patterns—one for front-end integration and the other for back-end integration. The diagram also shows that each Business and Integration pattern can be further made up of one or more Application patterns.

In Chapter 4 through Chapter 14, the first page shows a figure similar to the one in

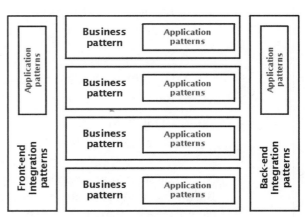

Figure 3.1: This pattern diagram is used throughout the rest of the book.

Figure 3.1, but with the Business and Integration pattern placeholders replaced by the respective pattern names. The shading in the figure indicates which part is the subject of the chapter. This will orient you to the content of each chapter as you read the book.

Witin each chapter, each new pattern is highlighted by a shaded heading.

Textual notation

The textual notation *Business pattern::Application pattern* is used to refer to an Application pattern documented elsewhere in this book. Thus, you will see references such as *Self-Service::Router application pattern* and *Extended Enterprise::Exposed Business Services application pattern*. This makes it easier for you to look for details of the referenced Application pattern.

For the capitalization scheme used for Patterns for e-business, refer to the "About this book" section preceding Chapter 1.

Standard descriptive framework

A standard framework is used throughout the following chapters for documenting the Patterns for e-business. This framework is consistent with earlier patterns efforts, and makes it easy to compare different patterns and evaluate them for use in your projects. The framework consists of eight sections:

1. Pattern name and brief description
2. Business and IT drivers
3. Context
4. Solution
5. Guidelines for use
6. Benefits
7. Limitations
8. Usage of the pattern

Not all these sections are relevant to each type of pattern, however. For example, Business and Integration patterns use sections 1 2, 3, 4, and 8, while Application patterns use sections 1, 2, 4, 5, 6, 7, and 8. The reasons for the missing sections are given in the following section descriptions.

Pattern name and brief description

In the first section of our standard framework, the name of the pattern is given in the header, followed by a brief description of it in the text. The name of the pattern creates a context and conveys a high-level description, while the description provides a quick summary of the pattern and its usage. This section also identifies any aliases that may exist for the pattern.

For an Integration pattern, the description section includes detailed descriptions of the individual services that need to be supported by the pattern.

Business and IT drivers

The second section lists the key criteria that influence the selection of a pattern for a given application. These decision criteria are a combination of the most commonly observed business and IT drivers or constraints that apply to a particular situation. The business and IT drivers are consistent when selecting a Business pattern, but vary when selecting an Application pattern within a Business pattern. The following are some business drivers you might see when Application patterns are discussed within a specific Business pattern:

- *Decrease the time to market.* One of the hallmarks of a good design is how it accelerates the implementation and facilitates the development and deployment of e-business solutions in a short amount of time. Application patterns that do this tend to minimize the changes to back-end systems and databases and reuse the back-end code. They also tend to reuse services in the middle tier and rely on proven and reliable technologies.

- *Improve the organizational efficiency.* e-business solutions help improve the efficiency of key processes within the application and thereby have a direct impact on the overall efficiency of the organization. Application designs that do this tend to focus heavily on the integration between components and the aggregation of information.

- *Reduce the latency of business events.* One way of improving organizational efficiency is to reduce the latency in business processes and events within a given application. This can be implemented by using streamlined workflows and providing closer integration between the components.

- *Provide a unified customer view across lines of business (LOB).* As the Web and other channels become more numerous, organizations must synchronize these channels to provide a uniform and consistent view of customer data. Applications that facilitate this unified customer view need to have components that collect and integrate data before transforming the data to suit a particular channel.

- *Enable easy adaptation during mergers and acquisitions.* To support the rapid deployment of business functions and adapt to a rapidly changing business environment, e-business solutions should be designed for high degrees of flexibility and adaptability. Some Application patterns lend themselves to greater adaptability and hence help facilitate the transition of systems and data that occur during mergers and acquisitions.

- *Support partnership with external entities*, while minimizing dependency on these entities. To implement highly integrated business processes that span multiple organizations and departments, it is critical that the solutions have a high degree of cohesion and a low level of coupling. This means that the applications that implement such processes should provide a seamless interface to the users of the solution, while minimizing the dependence between the entities. Successful application designs borrow heavily from the concept of "black-box" systems design, which focuses heavily on the exact specification of the interfaces that need to be established while hiding the details of the implementation.

The following are some IT drivers you might see in the discussion of Application patterns within a specific Business pattern:

- *Minimize total cost of ownership (TCO).* One of the major objectives of any solution is to look at the overall cost of ownership and understand the implications of these costs on the long-term viability of the solution. As they are developing new applications in the e-business arena, many organizations tend to take a short-term view, looking at the immediate costs of development or of procuring hardware and software. In many cases, they tend to overlook important back-end costs, such as code maintenance, support, and upgrading the technologies underlying the overall solution. One of the primary objectives of a good design and, by implication, the Application pattern that represents it, is to minimize the overall cost of ownership of the solution, not just the front-end procurement or development costs.

- *Leverage existing skills.* In the transition to a digital economy, there has been a massive increase in the demand for the skills needed to design, implement, and support e-business solutions. In addition, for e-business solutions to be truly effective, they need to be integrated with the back-end legacy systems and databases. A good Application pattern, therefore, strikes an effective balance between using the latest technologies and leveraging the skills that already exist in an organization.

- *Leverage legacy investment.* As mentioned earlier, e-business solutions need to be closely linked to the mission-critical back-end systems and databases that support the day-to-day operations of the organization. In addition, many organizations have invested millions of dollars in upgrading their legacy systems to be Y2K compliant. To recover the investments in this area, it makes good business sense for companies to continue to take full advantage of existing systems, applications, and data. Thus, all good Application patterns tend to leverage existing investments in legacy systems and take an approach of "modify and integrate" (in contrast to the "rip and replace" strategy promoted by many leading client/server vendors in the early 1990s).

- *Provide back-end integration.* To provide a positive and seamless user experience across multiple access channels (such as the Web, interactive voice-response units, client service representatives, and store sales representatives), it is important to integrate with the back-end applications and data.

- *Minimize complexity.* Speed, the ability to respond to changes in technology and business processes, and maintainability are the hallmarks of good e-business architectures. One of the critical things in making this happen is to stick to the old adage of "keeping it simple." Complexity in the architecture (such as custom-built application components or infrastructure components) minimizes the ability to respond to change, and therefore compromises speed. Good designs, therefore, tend to favor simplicity and the reuse of off-the-shelf components over complexity and custom-developed code.

- *Provide availability*. Because most e-business solutions cater to a customer base that extends beyond the boundaries of the organization, they should be available around the clock and minimize the amount of downtime. Good designs include redundancy of the services, hardware, and instrumentation needed to guarantee the availability of the application.

- *Provide scalability*. e-business solutions should support scalability across two major domains:

  - In the hardware domain, scalability is achieved by adding more servers (horizontal scalability) or by adding more powerful servers (vertical scalability).

  - In the software domain, scalability is achieved through redundant services, caching, and techniques that share valuable resources (such as connection pooling and thread pooling).

The business and IT drivers section of the framework uses a table similar to Table 3.1 to provide a quick overview of the drivers that influence the choice of a particular Application pattern.

Table 3.1: *Business and IT drivers for a particular Application pattern*

Business drivers	IT drivers
Decrease the time to market.	Minimize the TCO.
Improve organizational efficiency.	Leverage existing skills.
Reduce the latency of business events.	Leverage the legacy Investment.
Integrate across multiple delivery channels.	Integrate the back-end application.
Provide a unified customer view across LOB.	Minimize application complexity.
Support effective cross-selling.	Minimize enterprise complexity.
Provide mass customization.	Improve availability.
Enable easy adaptation during mergers and acquisitions.	Provide scalability.
Support partnership with external entities, while minimizing dependency on these entities.	Improve maintainability.

Context

The "Context" section describes situations in which the problem can be seen. It includes several practical examples showing the need for a pattern to solve the problem. This section is included for Business and Integration patterns, but omitted for Application patterns because the Business or Integration pattern parent provides the context for each Application pattern.

Solution

For Business and Integration patterns, a simple schematic is used to show the key participants involved in the pattern and the interaction between these participants. For Application patterns, the "Solution" section describes the topology of the required application. The major objective of the section is to identify the major components that are part of the Application pattern and identify the nature of the interactions between them (synchronous versus asynchronous). This section also captures the persistence of data and processes within the application topology, as shown in Figure 3.2.

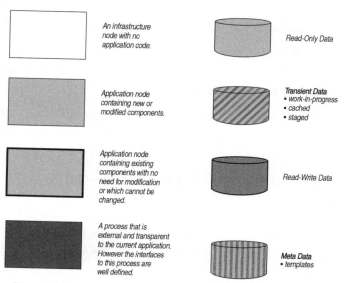

Figure 3.2: These symbols are used to represent Application patterns.

The diagrams in the "Solution" sections use a set of symbols to represent the overall structure of the application:

- A database symbol represents a data store within the application. This data store can be one of the following:

  - A read-only data store is represented by a lightly shaded database symbol. This data store cannot be modified or updated by the current application.

  - A transient data store used to store work-in-progress, cached, or replicated data, is represented by a hatched database symbol.

  - An application data store that supports read and write operations, is represented by a darkly shaded database symbol.

  - A meta data store, containing information about data, is represented by a database symbol with vertical lines.

- An application or process symbol represents application-processing functions within the application. This includes the following:

  - A plain rectangle represents an infrastructure node with no application code.

  - A lightly shaded rectangle represents a process or an application function that needs to be created or modified to support the application.

  - A lightly shaded rectangle with a thick border represents a process that is external to the application and cannot be modified within the context of the current application.

  - A darkly shaded rectangle represents a process that is external and transparent to the current application. However, the interfaces to this process are specified and defined in detail.

- A connector symbol (a line connecting a process symbol to another process symbol or to a database symbol), typically has a descriptor of synchronous or asynchronous to indicate whether the programmatic interaction between the adjacent tiers is implemented as a synchronous or asynchronous service request. The latter are defined as follows:

  - A synchronous service request is characterized by the fact that the server operation is synchronous with the requester operation, in the sense that, after the requester has issued a service request, it waits while the service is performed until the server confirms the success (or failure) of the request. (The synchronous/asynchronous nature of the service request is independent of the synchronous/asynchronous protocol used to carry the request.)

- An asynchronous service request is characterized by the fact that the server operation is asynchronous to the requester operation, in the sense that, after the requester has issued a service request, it does not wait, but continues immediately with other activities.

Guidelines for use

The "Guidelines for use" section identifies some typical scenarios or conditions that would influence an architect to use this pattern rather than another in his or her solution. This section is included for Application patterns, but not required for Business or Integration patterns because only one of these will typically match the Business or Integration problem being addressed.

Benefits

The "Benefits" section describes some of the reasons why this pattern should be considered for use in solutions. Note that this section should be used in conjunction with the "Limitations" section to make a good decision on the use of a pattern.

This section is included for Application patterns, but not required for Business or Integration patterns because only one of these will typically match the business or integration problem being addressed.

Limitations

The "Limitations" section describes some of the drawbacks or limitations that users should be aware of as they are evaluating the applicability of this pattern in their solutions. This section is included for Application patterns, but not required for Business or Integration patterns because only one of these will typically match the business or integration problem being addressed.

Putting the pattern to use

The "Putting the pattern to use" section describes a real-life situation where this pattern can be observed. This could include an example or an illustration of how the pattern is used in a solution.

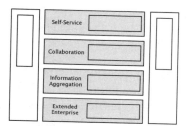

Business patterns

Business patterns are high-level constructs that can be used to describe the key business purpose of a solution. These patterns describe the objectives of the solution, the high-level participants who interact in the solution, and the nature of the interactions between the participants. Structurally, Business patterns are made up of two of the following three participants:

- The users of these solutions, who could include customers, investors, partners, and vendors.

- The enterprise or organization with which these users interact. This participant, called the business, could represent the organization as a whole or systems (applications or software programs) within the organization.

- The data that exists within an organization. Data is distinguished from applications and programs because the nature of interactions between these participants is very different.

The following four Business patterns, also listed in Figure 4.1, highlight the commonly observed interactions between users, businesses, and data:

- Self-Service (also known as User-to-Business)
- Collaboration (also known as User-to-User)
- Information Aggregation (also known as User-to-Data)
- Extended Enterprise (also known as Business-to-Business)

Note that the IBM patterns Web site previously used the aliases given in parentheses in the list, instead of the names used here. In keeping with our evolving thought processes, we intend to synchronize the nomenclature across all forms of communication (including the Web site, this book, and presentations) in the near future.

These four patterns, or subsets of these patterns, form the fundamental building blocks of most e-business solutions. They have the following characteristics:

- Each pattern is self-contained. The scope of each pattern embraces the minimum end-to-end flows necessary to implement an automated business process of this type. For example, the Self-Service business pattern includes the end-to-end transaction flow, security flow, and restart/recovery flow.

- Each pattern typically interacts with other patterns through one or more integration points, such as a file transfer, a message transfer, a common database, a common component, a common application, a common process, a common access point, or a common workflow.

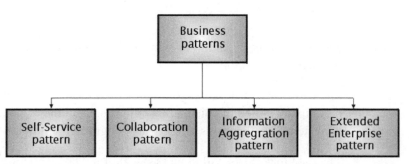

Figure 4.1: These four Business patterns are the foundation of most e-business solutions.

The consequence of the common characteristics is that today's complex solutions are built by combining the primary Business patterns described in this chapter using one or more Integration patterns (described in Chapter 5). This classification enables you to avoid the redundant definition of known patterns. It would be unrealistic to expect this simple taxonomy to cover all known applications, but we have found it to be a powerful approach for analyzing 80% of the common functions of 80% of common business applications.

~ The Self-Service business pattern

The Self-Service business pattern, also known as the User-to-Business or U2B pattern, captures the essence of direct interactions between interested parties and a business. Interested parties include customers, business partners, stakeholders, employees, and all other individuals with whom the business intends to interact. For simplicity, these interested parties are referred to as *users*. In this definition, *business* represents various types of organizations, including large enterprises, small and medium businesses, and government agencies.

Business and IT drivers

The business and IT drivers for this pattern are shown in Table 4.1.

Table 4.1: *Business and IT drivers for the Self-Service business pattern*

Business and IT drivers	
The end-users and customers need to directly interact with business processes.	✓
The business process needs to be integrated with existing business systems and information.	✓
The business processes need to be integrated with processes and information that exist at partner organizations.	
The business activity has a need to aggregate, organize, and present information from various sources within and outside of the organization.	
The business process must be reachable in a common, consistent, and simplified manner through multiple delivery channels.	✓
The business activity demands and fosters collaboration and the sharing of information among its participants.	

Context

The Self-Service business pattern is commonly observed in e-business solutions that provide users the ability to access their information and change it by interacting directly with core business systems and databases. This pattern captures the essence of direct interactions between users and the enterprise. Such interactions can range from simple, static, information lookup to complex updates involving enterprise data. Examples of applications that use the Self-Service business pattern include the following:

- Customer-facing applications such as an online broker application that allows investors to manage their portfolios and make equity trades across the Web

- Business-partner-facing applications such as a dealer extranet that allows dealers of a manufacturing company to link their sales and distribution operations to the shop-floor processes by exchanging forecast, demand, and production information

- Employee-facing human-resource applications such as time reporting, benefits processing, and expense submission

This Business pattern can be realized using several Application patterns based on the needs of the business process. These Application patterns are described in Chapter 7.

Solution

This pattern typically consists of the following:

- Users, who:

  - May be within the enterprise, in partner organizations, or in any other location across the globe.

  - Will typically access the solution using a Web browser or a browser-based Internet appliance. The enterprise has very little or no control over how this device is set up or configured. (Access from non-browser-based devices can be supported by adding pervasive device support patterns to the basic Self-Service patterns.)

  - Can access the solution from any location across the Internet.

- A network, which:

  - Is based on TCP/IP and other Internet technologies.

  - Can be a dedicated LAN connection, a broadband connection, or a dial-up connection.

- Enterprise systems, which can be:

  - Custom-developed systems (old and new).

  - ERP systems and other packaged applications such as SAP, BAAN, and PeopleSoft.

  - Databases.

- A set of interactions representing the business functions provided to users.

A schematic of the participants in the Self-Service business pattern is shown in Figure 4.2.

Figure 4.2: The Self-Service business pattern consists of these participants.

Putting the pattern to use

This pattern can be observed in solutions such as the following:

- Electronic brokerage sites that allow individual investors (users) to access and manage their portfolios (a set of interactions) by connecting to stock-quote, portfolio-management, and securities-trading systems (core business systems and databases) across the Internet (the network). An example is found at http://www.bmonesbittburns.com.

- Web-based retailers that allow customers to shop for and buy apparel, cosmetics, and other retail goods by accessing catalogs of items and order entry functions from their browsers across the Internet. Examples are found at http://www.abercrombie.com and http://www.macys.com.

Although these examples are typically composed of more than one primary business pattern, the Self-Service business pattern is at the core of these solutions.

∿ The Collaboration business pattern

The Collaboration business pattern, also known as the User-to-User or U2U pattern, addresses the interactions and collaborations between users. This pattern can be observed in solutions that support small or extended teams who need to work together to achieve a joint goal.

Business and IT drivers

The business and IT drivers for this pattern are shown in Table 4.2.

Table 4.2: *Business and IT drivers for the Collaboration business pattern*

Business and IT drivers	
The end-users and customers need to directly interact with business processes.	✓
The business process needs to be integrated with existing business systems and information.	
The business processes need to be integrated with processes and information that exist at partner organizations.	
The business activity has a need to aggregate, organize, and present information from various sources within and outside of the organization.	
The business process must be reachable in a common, consistent, and simplified manner through multiple delivery channels.	
The business activity demands and fosters collaboration and the sharing of information among its participants.	✓

Context

The Collaboration business pattern occurs in e-business solutions that involve one- or two-way interactions between users of the solution. These interactions can take many forms, including the following:

- Asynchronous collaboration, in which a user can address a message to another user or group of users on the network. This message is then sent to a collector (or container) where the intended recipient picks it up. This type of communication is typically seen in traditional e-mail systems based on SMTP (Simple Mail Transfer Protocol) and POP (Post Office Protocol) as well as in collaboration Web sites.

- Interactive collaboration, in which a user can collaborate with one or more users by sharing information synchronously. This type of communication is typically implemented through systems such as interactive chat rooms, bulletin boards, and instant messaging services.

- Broadcast and multicasting, in which a user can send a message or a sequence of messages to multiple recipients. This includes support for broadcasting rich media such as audio and video, and for streaming media.

The types of collaboration are often combined with a workflow engine that provides the ability to set up and sequence atomic activities to support more complex processes that may involve multiple users from different workgroups, departments, and organizations. This Business pattern can be realized using several Application patterns, based on the needs of the application. These Application patterns are described in Chapter 8.

Solution

This pattern typically consists of the following components:

- Users.

- A network that:
  - Is based on TCP/IP and other Internet technologies.
  - Can be a dedicated LAN connection, a broadband connection, or a dial-up connection.

- A set of collaboration services. These services can include support for:
  - A directory that will allow users to locate others on the network. This directory can also store the security and access privileges associated with each user.
  - Different types of data, from simple text to sophisticated, complex, large data elements, such as streaming audio and video.
  - Transient and persistent data sources that facilitate collaboration.

- A set of interactions that includes:
  - One-to-one, one-to-many, and many-to-many collaborations.
  - Simple and complex workflows involving a mix of users, programs, and applications.

A schematic of the participants in the Collaboration business pattern is shown in Figure 4.3.

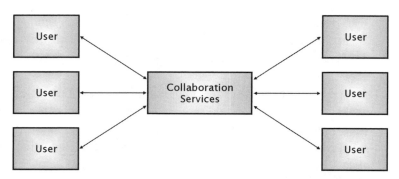

Figure 4.3: The Collaboration business pattern consists of these participants.

Putting the pattern to use

This pattern can be observed in solutions such as the following:

- Remote applications (such as Symantec's Anywhere) that allow remote users to connect to, interact with, and control remote systems and applications

- E-mail applications built on top of the IMAP or POP3 protocol that allow e-mail messages to be forwarded to and received from a server

- Shopping and interest clubs that are part of the latest online commerce sites

- Instant messaging provided by AOL to its users

The Information Aggregation business pattern

The Information Aggregation business pattern, also know as the User-to-Data or U2D pattern, can be observed in e-business solutions that allow users to access and manipulate data aggregated from multiple sources. This Business pattern captures the process of using tools to extract useful information from large volumes of data, text, images, video, and so on. These tools may personalize data to suit user preferences, distill summary information from large volumes of data, use algorithms to identify trends hidden in the data, or allow users to ask "'what-if'" questions.

Business and IT drivers

The business and IT drivers for this pattern are shown in Table 4.3.

Table 4.3: *Business and IT drivers for the Information Aggregation business pattern*

Business and IT drivers	
The end-users and customers need to directly interact with business processes and/or data..	✓
The business process needs to be integrated with existing business systems and information.	
The business processes need to be integrated with processes and information that exist at partner organizations.	
The business activity has a need to aggregate, organize, and present information from various sources within and outside of the organization.	✓
The business process must be reachable in a common, consistent, and simplified manner through multiple delivery channels.	
The business activity demands and fosters collaboration and the sharing of information among its participants.	

Context

Users of applications built according to the Information Aggregation business pattern might be internal or external to an organization. In both these cases, the objective is to transform raw data into useful information, for example:

- Business Intelligence (BI) applications typically focus on internal users such as executives, managers, and business analysts. BI applications are used to develop information that is conclusive, fact-based, and actionable. Such information is used to gain strategic insights and drive important business decisions.

- Portals that aggregate information from disparate data sources allow users to personalize this information to meet their preferences. There are many examples of such portals on the Web, including Yahoo and MSN.

Initially, you might find architectural similarities between applications that implement the Information Aggregation and the Self-Service business patterns. The two are distinguished, however, by the user's interaction with data versus a business transaction. Applications that implement the Information Aggregation business pattern facilitate direct interaction between users and data. These applications provide significant freedom and flexibility in accessing and manipulating data. This is one of the primary characteristics that differentiates this pattern from the Self-Service business pattern, which facilitates direct interaction between users and business transactions and processes.

Typically, applications that implement the Information Aggregation business pattern depend on applications that implement the Self-Service business pattern as the original source of much of the data. This is especially true because business activities are recorded on a minute-to-minute basis by applications that implement the Self-Service business pattern.

Designing applications that implement the Information Aggregation business pattern can be challenging for many reasons, including the fact that user requirements tend to be vague and constantly changing. Also, several applications can be built simultaneously, some with common data needs and others with conflicting needs. To overcome these challenges, best practice suggests that population and information-access functionality be separated in the design. This separation allows for greater flexibility in changing either the population function or the information-access function without affecting the other. This Business pattern can be realized using several Application patterns based on the needs of the application. These patterns are described in Chapter 9.

Solution

This pattern typically consists of the following:

- Users who:

  - Will have different preferences and want to access different views of the data.

  - Will typically access the solution using a Web browser or a browser-based Internet appliance. The enterprise has very little or no control over how this device is set up or configured.

  - Can access the solution from any location across the Internet.

- A network which:
    - Is based on TCP/IP and other Internet technologies.
    - Can be a dedicated LAN connection, a broadband connection, or a dial-up connection.
- Disparate data sources, such as:
    - Other Web sites and portals.
    - Core business systems.
    - Databases.
    - Other transient data sources.
- A set of interactions that includes:
    - Aggregating multiple sources of data.
    - Accessing distilled views of the data.

A schematic of the participants in the Information Aggregator business pattern is shown in Figure 4.4.

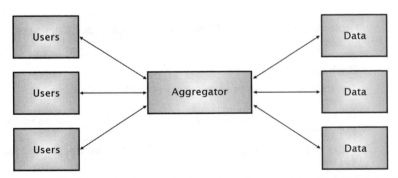

Figure 4.4: The Information Aggregation business pattern consists of these participants.

Putting the pattern to use

This pattern can be observed in solutions such as the following:

- Web sites for sporting events that allow millions of fans (users) to have real-time access to the latest news, scores, and results (data) from sporting events using various devices such as Web browsers, PDAs, and wireless phones (network). Examples are found at http://www.wimbledon.com and http://www.olympics.org.

- Internet (network) portals that aggregate information from disparate core business data sources (data) and allow thousands of users (users) to personalize this information to meet their preferences. Examples are found at http://www.yahoo.com and http://www.cnbc.com.

The Extended Enterprise business pattern

The Extended Enterprise business pattern, also know as the Business-to-Business or B2B pattern, addresses the interactions and collaborations between business processes in separate enterprises. This pattern can be observed in solutions that implement programmatic interfaces to connect inter-enterprise applications. In other words, it does not cover applications that are directly invoked through a user interface by business partners across organizational boundaries.

Business and IT drivers

The business and IT drivers for this pattern are shown in Table 4.4.

Table 4.4: *Business and IT drivers for the Extended Enterprise business pattern*

Business and IT drivers	
The end-users and customers need to directly interact with business processes.	
The business process needs to be integrated with existing business systems and information.	✓
The business processes need to be integrated with processes and information that exist at partner organizations.	✓
The business activity has a need to aggregate, organize, and present information from various sources within and outside of the organization.	
The business process must be reachable in a common, consistent, and simplified manner through multiple delivery channels.	
The business activity demands and fosters collaboration and the sharing of information among its participants.	

Context

Consider an online travel agency that enables customers to make travel arrangements. Customers can choose from a wide variety of accommodation options, including resorts, hotel chains, and small bed-and-breakfast establishments. The travel agency requires that all participating major business partners, such as resorts and hotel chains, provide programmatic interfaces that can be invoked in real time for checking room availability and making reservations. This is a classic example of business-to-business programmatic integration.

Conversely, small bed-and-breakfasts usually cannot afford to provide such programmatic interfaces to their reservation systems. To accommodate these business partners, the travel Web site provides a user interface that can be accessed by operators of bed-and-breakfasts to manually enter room availability into the system. Such user-interface-based interactions between partners are not covered under this pattern. (They can be modeled using the Self-Service business pattern discussed earlier in this chapter.) Instead, the general problem addressed by this pattern is illustrated in Figure 4.5.

Interactions between partners form a public process, or potentially, multiple distinct public processes. Each of these must be integrated into the private business process flows implemented by each partner. Such integration might be as simple as passing data to a particular application, or as sophisticated as initiating or resuming a multi-step workflow involving several applications and user interactions.

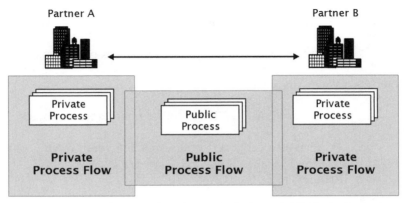

Figure 4.5: The B2B problem is addressed by the Extended Enterprise business pattern.

Examine Figure 4.5 and consider this scenario: Partner A and Partner B agree to share specific business processes and a process flow. Partner A invokes a public process flow that, in turn, may invoke a specific private internal process flow within Partner B's organization. Partner A is not concerned with the details of Partner B's private process flow. Instead, Partner A cares only about the results it expects in response to the invoked public process. The golden rule of business-to-business integration is the less you know about the business partner's private processes and the implementation details of their applications, the better off you are. This allows for loose coupling between partner applications. Such loose coupling enables business partners to evolve their applications without affecting each other's applications.

Obviously, specific functionality supported by these applications depends on the particular details of the trading partner agreements and service-level agreements between the organizations involved. Yet, a survey of such applications in multiple industries reveals certain common approaches that have been successful. The Application patterns that can be used to implement this Business pattern are described in Chapter 10.

Solution

This pattern may consist of all or some of the following elements:

- Business participants, which typically:
  - Are programs, applications, or databases that exist within an organization.
  - Access and connect to other business participants across the network.
- A network which:
  - Is based on TCP/IP and other Internet technologies.
  - Can be a dedicated Wide Area Network (WAN) connection.
- Business rules that:
  - Manage the integration between the business participants.
  - Describe Trading Partner Agreements (TPAs).

- Use workflow rules to determine the sequence of steps and the data flow that needs to be used to facilitate the integration. These rules:

  ✓ Describe the sequence of steps that a message needs to go through before being transferred to the other business participant.

  ✓ Specify how and where the message should be delivered.

- Transformation rules that specify the format and protocol transformations to be applied to messages that flow between the business participants.

- A set of interactions that includes the execution of a jointly agreed business process.

A schematic of the participants in the Extended Enterprise business pattern is shown in Figure 4.6.

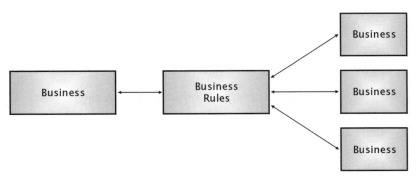

Figure 4.6: The Extended Enterprise business pattern consists of these participants.

Putting the pattern to use

This pattern can be observed in solutions such as the following:

- Business-to-business procurement sites that implement a series of workflows to facilitate the electronic procurement of goods and services. An example is found at http://stapleslink.com.

- Extended value-chain functions within e-marketplaces that support cross-enterprise processes such as demand planning and collaborative design.

Step 3: Identify Business patterns in the FECS solution

Refer back to the Solution Overview Diagram developed for the FutureStep Electronics Customer Service (FECS) solution in Chapter 2. Taking a closer look at this solution with the knowledge of Business patterns and their characteristics, you can identify the following patterns in the solution:

- The Self-Service business pattern can be observed where the customer accesses functions such as customer registration and preferences, and again where the customer accesses product selection, order entry, and inventory control.

- The Collaboration business pattern can be observed where the customer-notification function enables two-way e-mail and interfaces with PDAs and pagers.

- The Information Aggregation business pattern can be observed in the product-research forum that integrates data from multiple core business data sources, such as the product knowledge base and Web sites, and presents it to the customer as and when it is requested.

- The Extended Enterprise business pattern can be observed where the financing function integrates with external financial institutions.

You can now create a simple list of the Business patterns that occur in the solution. For the FECS solution, this list is shown in Figure 4.7.

You can also draw up a Solution Overview Diagram to depict the Business patterns within the solution. Figure 4.8 uses shaded boxes to identify the Business patterns in the FECS solution.

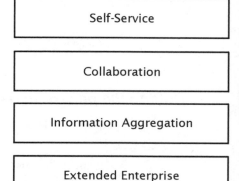

Figure 4.7: The pattern diagram for FECS illustrates its Business patterns.

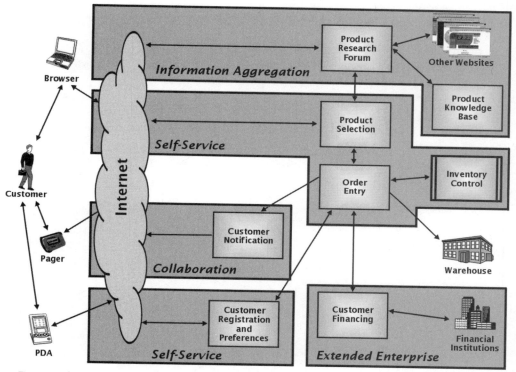

Figure 4.8: These are the Business patterns in FECS.

This picture appears to suggest that the Business patterns exist independently of one another, and do not interact or interface with one another. This is not true—which brings us to a new type of pattern, the Integration pattern, described in the next chapter.

C H A P T E R **5**

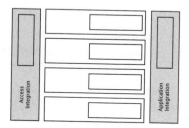

Integration patterns

T he following scenarios can be found in many domains of business or public
service:

- An online investor wishes to see a unified view of his/her net worth, which
  includes a summary of equities, mutual funds, and other financial
  instruments.

- A travel agent wants to make a single booking that combines reservations
  for airlines, hotels, and cars.

- A customer service representative wishes to view the contact and business
  information about a client and explain this information through instant
  messaging with the client.

- A user of a portal service needs to have access to multiple information
  sources and services, all personalized to role, privileges, and preferences.

- A company's purchase request is routed to the shop floor of a supplier and is
  integrated seamlessly into the manufacturing schedule and the invoicing and
  logistics (transportation) applications at the supplier with close to immediate
  commitment by the supplier to deliver.

Common among these scenarios is the need to integrate multiple applications,
modes of access, and sources of information. If you inspect a number of complex

e-business systems across different industries, you will see a commonality in their design. This commonality is expressed by Integration patterns.

Integration patterns differ from the rest of the patterns in this book in that they do not, by themselves, automate specific business problems. First, they are used within Business patterns to support more advanced functions. Second, they make custom designs and Composite patterns feasible by allowing the integration of two or more Business patterns. (Custom designs and Composite patterns are more fully defined in the next chapter.)

An inspection of the systems implementing integration reveals two major categories of recurring Integration patterns:

- Those that enable the user to access a multitude of services and information through a common portal, using a range of devices. This category is referred to as Access Integration patterns.

- Those aimed at integrating multiple applications and information sources without being directly invoked by the user. This category is referred to as Application Integration patterns.

The Access Integration pattern

The Access Integration pattern describes recurring designs that enable access to one or more Business patterns. In particular, this pattern enables access from multiple channels (devices) and integrates the common services required to support a consistent user interface.

Business and IT drivers

The business and IT drivers for this pattern are shown in Table 5.1.

Table 5.1: *Business and IT drivers for the Access Integration pattern*

Business and IT drivers	
The end-users and customers need to directly interact with business processes.	✓
The business process needs to be integrated with existing business systems and information.	
The business processes need to be integrated with processes and information that exist at partner organizations.	
The business activity has a need to aggregate, organize, and present information from various sources within and outside of the organization.	✓
The business process must be reachable in a common, consistent, and simplified manner through multiple delivery channels.	✓
The business activity demands and fosters collaboration and the sharing of information among its participants.	

Context

The Access Integration pattern is commonly observed in e-business solutions that provide users a seamless and consistent user experience that combines access to multiple applications, databases, and services. It can be thought of as a front-end integration pattern. This pattern is also observed when information needs to be presented via multiple delivery channels (devices). Access Integration patterns do not stand alone in a solution; they typically combine Business patterns to create the custom designs and Composite patterns that are used to solve complex business problems.

The Access Integration pattern can be realized using several Application patterns based on the needs of the business process. These Application patterns are described in Chapter 11.

Solution

This pattern typically consists of the following:

- Users, who:

  - May be within the enterprise, in partner organizations, or in any other location across the globe.

  - Will typically access the solution using a Web browser or a browser-based Internet appliance. The enterprise has very little or no control over how this device is set up or configured.

  - Can access the solution from any location across the Internet.

- A network, which

  - Is based on TCP/IP and other Internet technologies.

  - Can be a dedicated LAN connection, a broadband connection, or a dial-up connection.

- Business applications and data, which can be:

  - Custom developed systems (old and new).

  - ERP systems and other packaged applications, such as SAP, BAAN and PeopleSoft.

  - Databases.

- Access integration services that can include one or more of the following services:

  - Device support.

  - Presentation.

  - Personalization.

  - Security and administration.

A schematic of the participants in the Access Integration pattern is shown in Figure 5.1.

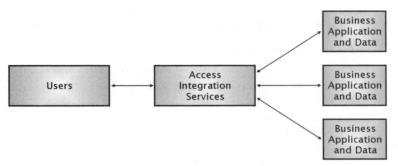

Figure 5.1: The Access Integration pattern consists of these participants.

Putting the pattern to use

This pattern can be observed in solutions such as the following:

- Customer-facing solutions, such as the online stores at http://www.avon.com and http://www.nuskin.com, which provide a personalized user interface that can be customized by the users to suit their requirements.

- Online portals, such as http://www.aol.com, which allows users to customize their interactions with the portal and specify their preferences for multiple access devices such as browsers, custom clients, PDAs, Web-enabled phones, and interactive set-top boxes.

The Application Integration pattern

Application Integration patterns are typically observed in solutions that call for the integration of Web-based solutions to core business systems and databases. This category of patterns can be mapped directly to the designs observed in the domain of Enterprise Application Integration (EAI). The requirements that gave rise to this pattern call for the seamless execution of multiple applications and access to their respective data in order to automate a complex, new business function.

Business and IT drivers

The business and IT drivers for this pattern are shown in Table 5.2.

Table 5.2: *Business and IT drivers for the Application Integration pattern*	
Business and IT drivers	
The end-users and customers need to directly interact with business processes.	
The business process needs to be integrated with existing business systems and information.	✓
The business processes need to be integrated with processes and information that exist at partner organizations.	✓
The business activity has a need to aggregate, organize, and present information from various sources within and outside of the organization.	✓
The business process must be reachable in a common, consistent, and simplified manner through multiple delivery channels.	
The business activity demands and fosters collaboration and the sharing of information among its participants.	

Context

Application Integration patterns can be observed in solutions that call for close integration with the systems and databases that exist within the organization or across organizational boundaries. Application Integration patterns can be thought of as back-end integration patterns. These patterns are critical for the successful implementation of some Business patterns. For example, it is hard to conceive of a solution that uses the Self-Service business pattern or an Extended Enterprise business pattern without using the Application Integration pattern within it. Similarly, it is hard to think of custom designs and Composite patterns (described in Chapter 6) existing without Application Integration patterns.

Application Integration patterns can be classified according to the following four attributes:

- By the function or work they perform:
  - Message pass-through
  - Message routing
  - Message enhancement
  - Message workflow

- By the focus of integration:
  - Data
  - Process (or message)

- By the mode of connection deployed:
  - Asynchronous
  - Synchronous

- By the targeted topology:
  - Point-to-point
  - Multi-point

A limited number of combinations of the above characteristics are found in some selected Application Integration patterns. These are described in Chapter 12, together with a description of the services required and relevant examples.

Solution

This pattern typically consists of the following:

- Business applications and data that need to communicate, interact, and integrate with other business applications and data either within the organization or in partner organizations

- A network, which:

  - Is based on TCP/IP and other Internet technologies

  - Can be a dedicated LAN connection or WAN connection

- Other business applications and data, which can be:

  - Custom-developed systems (old and new)

  - Enterprise Resource Planning systems and other packaged applications, such as SAP, BAAN and PeopleSoft

  - Databases

- Application integration services, which include:
  - Protocol adapters
  - Message handlers
  - Data transformation
  - Decomposition/recomposition

- Routing/navigation
- State management
- Security
- Local business logic
- (Business) unit-of-work management

A schematic of the participants in the Application Integration pattern is shown in Figure 5.2.

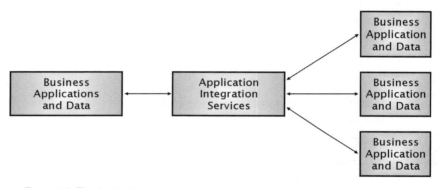

Figure 5.2: The Application integration pattern consists of these participants.

Putting the pattern to use

This is probably one of the most common patterns. It can be observed in any solution where an application needs to integrate with other applications, legacy systems, and databases, or with applications and processes in external organizations. Here are some examples:

- Any online store, such as http://www.macys.com or http://www.abercrombie.com, needs to integrate the online shopping process with core business systems and databases such as the inventory management system and an order-fulfillment system.

- Many Web sites syndicate content from content providers and integrate this content into their own sites. For instance, many Web sites offer driving directions by integrating into http://www.mapquest.com. In this case, the individual solutions are integrated with an application that exists outside the organization.

Step 4: Identify Integration patterns in the FECS solution

The previous step, in Chapter 4, shows how to modify the Solution Overview Diagram (SOD) to show the Business patterns that can be observed in the solution. In the current step, you first look at each of the lines between the functions and determine how the integration will be accomplished. In most cases, it will be done using the Application Integration pattern.

Second, you should understand the relationships between the Business patterns that have been identified within the solution. Functions that need to be tied together to provide a consistent experience to the user indicate the occurrence of an Access Integration pattern.

Taking a closer look at the SOD, you can see Application Integration patterns that link:

- The order entry function and the customer financing function

- The order entry function and the core business inventory-control system

- The order entry function and the customer notification function

- The customer registration function and the order entry function

- The product selection function and the product research forum function

In addition, you can also see the need for an Access Integration pattern that will:

- Provide users with direct access to multiple Business patterns, specifically the two Self-Service business patterns and the Information Aggregation business pattern

- Provide users with a seamless and consistent experience

- Combine access to other functions provided by the solution

- Deliver information to and facilitate communications with different devices, including PDAs and pagers

The Business and Integration patterns can now be combined into a pattern diagram representing a custom design, shown in Figure 5.3. This diagram is the basis for starting the discussion in Chapter 6.

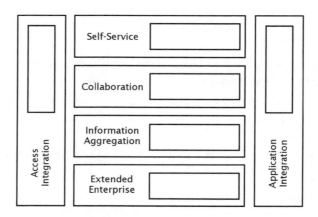

Figure 5.3: This pattern diagram illustrates a custom design for FECS.

Next, you can extend the SOD by drawing ellipses to indicate the Integration patterns, as shown in Figure 5.4. As you can see from the SOD, Integration patterns can occur in two distinct forms:

- To combine multiple Business patterns to form a solution. For instance, an Application Integration pattern connects the Self-Service pattern used for order entry and the Extended Enterprise pattern used for customer financing.

- Within a specific Business pattern. For example, an Application Integration pattern links the order entry function to the back-end inventory control system within the construct of the Self-Service business pattern.

At the same time, an Application Integration pattern does not link the order entry and product selection functions because we have made an assumption that these two functions are part of the same application, and hence will communicate with one another through some inter-program communication mechanism (like a sub-routine call or a remote procedure call). Similarly, the links from the product-research forum to the product-knowledge base and the other Web sites will also be handled by the appropriate Web-crawler package.

You might notice that there is no Application Integration pattern linking the order entry function to the warehouse. This is because the case study describes this link as via e-mail, which is already available using the order entry link to the collaborative customer notification function.

This diagram will be refined further in later chapters of the book during the solution development process, by breaking the Business patterns down into their appropriate Application patterns.

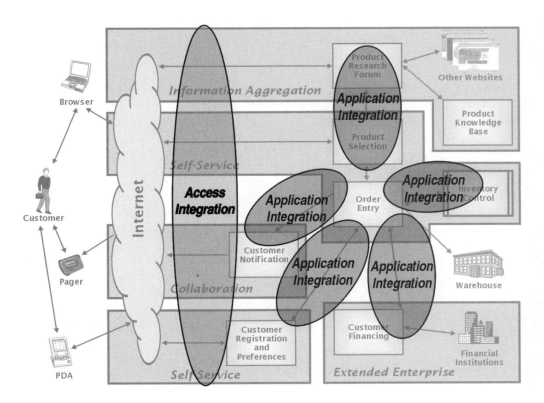

Figure 5.4: Integration patterns are added to the FECS Solution Overview Diagram.

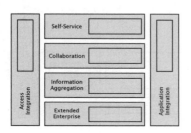

Composite patterns

So far, the following four Business patterns have been described in this book as necessary and sufficient to solve a basic business problem:

- Self-Service

- Collaboration

- Information Aggregation

- Extended Enterprise

In effect, each of these patterns offers a reuse strategy for solving a basic business problem from end to end.

Custom designs and Composite patterns

Whenever more than one Business pattern is needed to solve a business problem, an Integration pattern must be included so that the solution can be simplified or made seamless to the user or application requiring the solution. Chapter 5 identifies two Integration patterns:

- Access Integration

- Application Integration

Custom designs

These Business and Integration patterns can be combined, much like Lego blocks, to implement installation-specific business solutions. A pattern diagram representing such a custom design is shown in Figure 6.1. When a particular Business or Integration pattern is not used in a solution, it will not be shown in the pattern diagram.

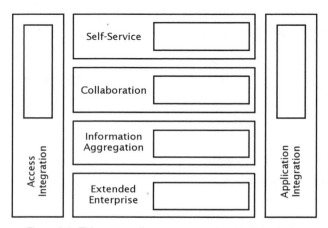

Figure 6.1: This pattern diagram represents a custom design.

Composite patterns

As solutions to more and more complex problems are assembled, you will begin to see the recurrence of certain combinations of Business and Integration patterns. For instance, most solutions today provide a personalized user experience. These solutions also typically expose key functions of line-of-business applications by integrating with them. Therefore, in most of these solutions, you will observe an Access Integration pattern, a Self-Service business pattern, and an Application Integration pattern. This generic combination of patterns is called a *Composite pattern*.

Extending the Patterns for e-business

Composite patterns represent commonly occurring combinations of Business patterns and Integration patterns. These Composite patterns typically solve major portions of functionality within a solution. The diagram in Figure 6.2 can be used with appropriate shading to show a Composite pattern. Bold text and boxes represent Business and Integration patterns that will always be included in the Composite pattern, while gray text and boxes represent Business and Integration patterns that can be optionally added to create variations on the Composite pattern. When a particular Business or Integration pattern is rarely used, it will not be shown in the Composite pattern.

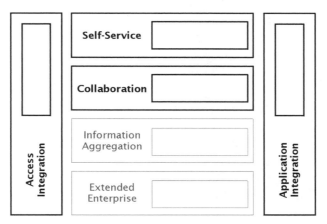

Figure 6.2: This diagram is an example of a Composite pattern.

Now, take a closer look at some of the most commonly observed Composite patterns.

Electronic commerce composite pattern

In the early days of our work on the Patterns for e-business, we described a fifth Business pattern called User-to-Online-Buying. Readers familiar with the Patterns for e-business Web site published in November 1999 will have seen a reference to this pattern and recognize that it was used primarily in Electronic Commerce applications.

In retrospect, we believe it is more accurate to describe an Electronic Commerce application as a Composite pattern because it is better represented by a combination of Business patterns and Integration patterns. The Composite pattern for an Electronic Commerce solution will consist of the following:

- A Self-Service business pattern that provides customers access to Web site functions such as browsing a catalog, placing an order, and making a payment

- An Information Aggregation pattern that aggregates information from multiple sources into a unified catalog of items

- An Application Integration pattern that combines the Self-Service pattern and the Information Aggregation pattern to provide a unified solution to the customer

Electronic Commerce solutions can have several optional variants, including the following:

- An Access Integration pattern that provides for more sophisticated functions, such as personalization and pervasive device access, aimed at increasing the user-friendliness of the site

- A Collaboration business pattern that provides functions such as automatic order confirmation through e-mail or online chat capabilities with customer service representatives

- An Extended Enterprise pattern that can be used to implement a direct connection with the shipping company that delivers the order to the customer

The Composite pattern for Electronic Commerce solutions is shown in Figure 6.3.

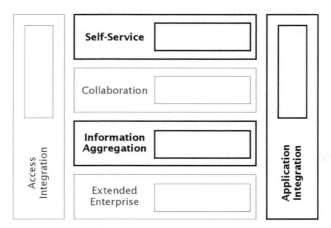

Figure 6.3: The Electronic Commerce composite pattern can have several variants.

An example of an application where the Electronic Commerce composite pattern occurs is http://www.macys.com.

Portal composite pattern

A portal solution is typically designed to aggregate multiple information sources and applications to provide uniform, seamless, and personalized access for its users. There are many variations of portal applications. The Composite pattern for portal applications is made up of an Access Integration pattern that facilitates functions such as single sign-on, multiple device support, and personalization, plus at least one other Business pattern. This Composite pattern is shown in Figure 6.4.

There are many variants to a portal application. Two of the most common are an Enterprise Intranet portal and a Collaboration ASP portal.

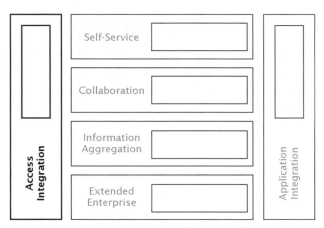

Figure 6.4: This diagram represents a Composite pattern for portals.

Enterprise intranet portal composite pattern

An Enterprise Intranet portal provides self-service functions that give access to human resource applications such as payroll, benefits, and travel expenses. In addition, this type of portal aggregates content from various sources and provides seamless access to this content. Finally, many Enterprise Intranet portals provide collaboration functions such as virtual help desks, e-mail, and instant messaging.

The Composite pattern for the Enterprise Intranet portal is shown in Figure 6.5. An example of such a portal is IBM's intranet at http://w3.ibm.com.

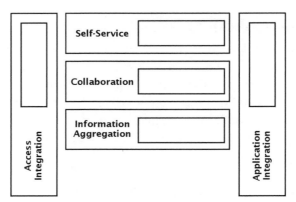

Figure 6.5: This diagram represents a Composite pattern for an Enterprise Intranet portal.

Collaboration ASP composite pattern

A Collaboration Application Service Provider (ASP) typically provides Internet users access to a particular type of collaboration solution, such as e-mail or instant messaging. The Composite pattern for a Collaboration ASP is shown in Figure 6.6. Examples of such a portal are found at http://www.centra.com and http://www.hotmail.com.

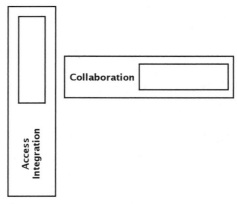

Figure 6.6: This diagram represents a Composite pattern for a Collaboration ASP.

≈ Account access composite pattern

Account Access solutions provide customers around-the-clock access to their account information. They also allow users to inquire about, update, and delete information in their individual accounts. Many applications fall under this category of solutions; they range from trading applications provided by online brokerages to account manager functions provided by utilities such as telephone companies. This category of solutions also includes account access applications provided by banks, credit card companies, and insurance companies.

The Composite pattern for an Account Access solution, shown in Figure 6.7, consists of the following:

- An Access Integration pattern that provides a unified mechanism to implement single sign-on capabilities. This pattern also provides a personalized experience to the account holder.

- A Self-Service business pattern that provides access to information stored in core business systems and databases.

- Optionally, an Information Aggregation pattern in cases where information from multiple accounts is summarized to provide a single unified portfolio view to the customer.

- Optionally, a Collaboration business pattern for functions such as online chat with a customer service representative and help desk support.

If the solution has any one of the optional Business patterns, it may also include an Application Integration pattern to seamlessly combine the Business patterns. An example of the Account Access solution is found at http://www.amica.com.

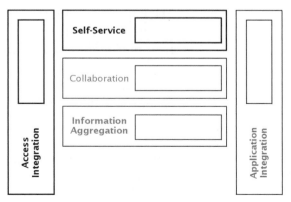

Figure 6.7: This diagram represents a Composite pattern for an Account Access solution.

e-Marketplaces

e-Marketplaces are trading exchanges that facilitate and promote buying, selling, and business communities among trading partners within certain industries. These solutions represent some of the most comprehensive and complex e-business applications today. There are three types of e-Marketplaces:

- Trading Exchange
- Sell-Side Hub
- Buy-Side Hub

∼ Trading exchange composite pattern

A Trading Exchange allows buyers and sellers to trade goods and services on a public site. The Composite pattern for a Trading Exchange consists of the following:

- The Self-Service business pattern facilitates the interaction between the buyer and the e-Marketplace. Activities such as purchasing from an aggregated catalog, participating in auctions, or making exchanges are performed using this pattern.

- The Self-Service business pattern also helps the non-commerce seller perform functions such as updating the catalog, checking orders, checking for requests for quotations, and accessing orders.

- The Information Aggregation business pattern is used to create the e-Marketplace catalog from multiple sources, such as suppliers' product files, pricing files, and advertising literature.

- The Application Integration pattern is used to integrate these two business patterns seamlessly. It is also used to integrate with existing e-Marketplace support systems, like billing.

- The Access Integration pattern is used to provide a Portal interface, single sign-on functions, and personalization functions for the e-Marketplace.

In addition to these basic functions, many additional functions can be added to an e-Marketplace as it evolves, such as the following:

- The Collaboration business pattern can be used to enable the purchasing approval process.

- The Extended Enterprise business pattern can be used on both the buyer and seller sides of the e-Marketplace. On the buyer side, the pattern defines the interaction between the buyer's procurement system and the commerce functions of the e-Marketplace. On the seller side, the pattern defines the interaction between the procurement functions of the e-Marketplace and its suppliers.

Figure 6.8 shows the Composite pattern for Trading Exchanges.

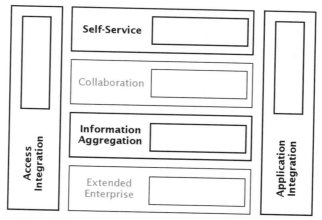

Figure 6.8: This diagram represents a Composite Pattern for Trading Exchanges.

∼ Sell-Side Hub composite pattern

In a Sell-Side Hub, the seller owns the e-Marketplace and uses it as a vehicle to sell goods and services to prospective buyers across the Web. The Composite pattern for the Sell-Side Hub, shown in Figure 6.9, includes the following:

- An Access Integration pattern that helps provide a unified customer interface

- A Self-Service business pattern that allows users to browse through a catalog, create an order, and place an order with the hub

- An Information Aggregation business pattern that is used to create the e-Marketplace catalog from the multiple sources of suppliers' product files, pricing files, and advertising literature

- Application Integration patterns to integrate the Business patterns that are part of the Sell-Side Hub

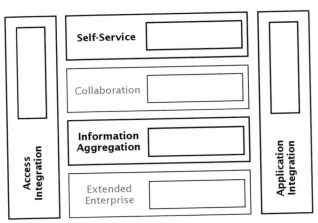

Figure 6.9: This diagram represents a Composite pattern for a Sell-Side Hub.

In addition to these basic functions, there can be several variations on this pattern, including the following:

- A Collaboration business pattern can be added to enable auctions, reverse auctions, and other collaborative buying functions.

- An Information Aggregation business pattern can be added to help integrate and present a unified catalog that combines raw catalog data with expert advice, product comparisons, and recommendations pulled off public Internet sites.

- An Extended Enterprise business pattern can be added to integrate the Sell-Side Hub with external service providers, such as a financial institution to handle credit processing or a shipping company to handle the physical delivery of goods.

∼ Buy-Side Hub composite pattern

In a Buy-Side Hub, the buyer of goods owns the e-Marketplace and uses it as a vehicle to leverage the buying or procurement budget in soliciting the best deals for goods and services from prospective sellers across the Web. The Composite pattern for the Buy-Side Hub, shown in Figure 6.10, includes the following:

- An Access Integration pattern that helps provide a unified customer sign-on capability and a personalized user interface

- A Collaboration business pattern that allows users to post bids, participate in auctions, and respond to requests for proposals (RFPs) and requests for quotations (RFQs)

- A Self-Service business pattern that allows buyers to create RFQs and RFPs

- Application Integration patterns that integrate the Buy-Side Hub with procurement systems and other core business applications

In addition to these basic functions, there can be several variations on this pattern, including these:

- An Information Aggregation business pattern can be added to help integrate content sources across the Web.

- An Extended Enterprise business pattern can be added to integrate the Buy-Side Hub with external service providers such as financial institutions.

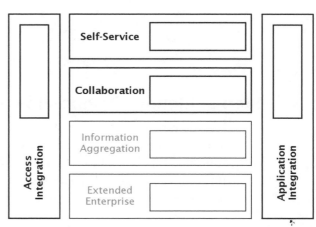

Figure 6.10: This diagram represents a Composite pattern for a Buy-Side Hub.

The continual evolution of Composite patterns

As e-business solutions and their underlying business models continue to evolve, newer Composite patterns will probably emerge. By analyzing a proposed business model, it should be possible to assemble a combination of Business and Integration patterns into a custom design that can deliver the business functions required. If the same design is adopted by multiple installations, it might become a Composite pattern.

In the meantime, many of today's commonly occurring e-business solutions can be described adequately using the Composite patterns in this chapter. Table 6.1 provides some examples.

Table 6.1: *Composite and Business patterns that make up common e-business solutions*	
Solution	Composite and Business Patterns that make up the solution
Online stores	Electronic Commerce
Auction sites	Electronic Commerce Collaboration
Online account managers	Account Access
Commercial portals	Portals Account Access Electronic Commerce
e-Markets	e-Marketplaces Sell-Side Hubs

Step 5: Identify Composite patterns in the FECS solution

We can now look at the Solution Overview Diagram to identify the Composite patterns that occur in the case study. This step is very useful when the executives responsible for the solution wish to implement major portions of the business function using software packages. However, developing a detailed architecture requires refinements using the process defined in later chapters of this book.

It is important for designers to go through all the steps of this process, even if the solution will be implemented using vendor packages. This will help define the Application and Runtime patterns that will provide the service-level characteristics (such as availability, scalability, and performance) expected from the solution. It

will also help the executives make informed decisions and have reasonable service-level expectations for these packages.

Recall that the FECS solution needs to allow the user to browse an electronic catalog and create an order by selecting items from the catalog. Then, FECS needs to
allow users to pay for the order. This functionality of the solution can be implemented using the Electronic Commerce composite pattern. It is also possible to implement additional business requirements such as the following, using variations of
the Electronic Commerce composite pattern:

- Integrating with the existing inventory control application
- Integrating with an external customer registration and personalization
  function
- Notifying the customer and e-mailing the order to the warehouse
- Supporting the product research forum and related functions
- Supporting the customer financing function
- Providing a portal interface

This is shown in Figure 6.11.

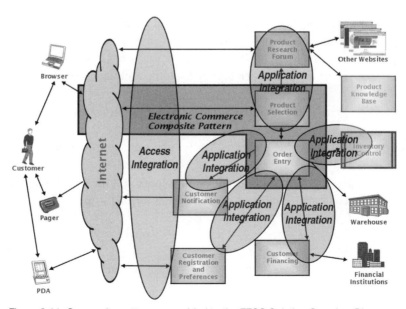

Figure 6.11: Composite patterns are added to the FECS Solution Overview Diagram.

Based on this observation, it is safe to assume that the solution might need to use an Electronic Commerce package such as WebSphere Commerce Suite. (As Electronic Commerce packages mature, they can be expected to support more and more possible variations of the Electronic Commerce composite pattern.) However, as mentioned earlier, the solution should be refined further using the steps outlined in subsequent chapters before a final decision is made. This will allow you to pick packages and products that implement the right Application patterns, and that "snap together," integrating well to provide the expected service-level characteristics. If the Composite patterns identified do not meet your needs, you can always compose a custom design using the appropriate Business and Integration patterns.

We have now completed the business-level analysis that needs to be done to develop a solution using the Patterns for e-business. The next step is to determine the Application patterns that can be used to automate the Business and Integration patterns identified so far in the case study. The business and IT drivers of FutureStep Electronics influence the selection of the appropriate Application pattern. Such a selection is also substantiated by additional business and technical requirements. Hence, supporting business and technical requirements about the processes, applications, and databases in FutureStep Electronics need to be gathered. These requirements will answer questions such as the following:

- What systems exist in the current IT environment, who owns them, and where are they hosted?

- How adaptable are legacy systems and databases?

- What is the nature of interactions supported by these systems and databases?

- What are the expected traffic and transaction volumes?

Examples of these additional requirements and the FECS technical context are examined as part of the case study in Chapters 7 through 12.

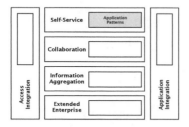

C H A P T E R 7

Application patterns for Self-Service

T he Self-Service business pattern captures the essence of direct interactions between interested parties and a business. These interactions can range from a simple information lookup to the execution of a complex business process. The specific business functionality supported by applications that automate the Self-Service business pattern varies from one industry to another. A survey of such applications in multiple industries reveals, however, that certain common approaches have been successful.

The Self-Service business pattern

In this chapter, these approaches are captured by the seven Application patterns shown in Figure 7.1. In addition, this chapter documents criteria by which you might evaluate these Application patterns for adoption in your own projects.

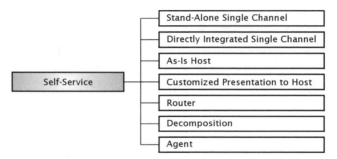

Figure 7.1: These seven Application patterns are widely successful for automating the Self-Service business pattern.

When reading this chapter, keep in mind that the Application patterns are *logical* constructs that may be *physically* implemented in different ways. For example, an Application pattern with three logical tiers may be implemented as two, three, or four physical tiers.

Summary of business and IT drivers for Self-Service

Tables 7.1 and 7.2 summarize the business and IT drivers for each Application pattern described in this chapter.

Table 7.1: *Business drivers for Self-Service application patterns*

Business drivers	Stand-alone Single Channel	Directly Integrated Single Channel	As-Is Host	Customized Presentation to Host	Router	Decomposition	Agent
Decrease the time to market.	✓		✓	✓			
Improve the organizational efficiency.		✓	✓	✓		✓	✓
Reduce the latency of business events.	✓				✓	✓	✓
Enable easy adaptation during mergers and acquisitions.					✓	✓	✓
Integrate across multiple delivery channels.					✓	✓	✓
Provide a unified customer view across lines of business (LOB).						✓	✓
Support effective cross-selling.							✓
Support mass customization.							✓

Table 7.2: *IT drivers for Self-Service application patterns*

IT drivers	Stand-Alone Single Channel	Directly Integrated Single Channel	As-Is Host	Customized Presentation to host	Router	Decomposition	Agent
Minimize the application's complexity.	✓			✓			
Minimize the total cost of ownership (TCO).		✓	✓	✓	✓	✓	✓
Leverage existing skills.	✓	✓	✓	✓	✓	✓	✓
Leverage the legacy investment.	✓	✓	✓	✓	✓	✓	✓
Provide back-end application integration.	✓	✓	✓	✓	✓	✓	✓
Minimize the enterprise's complexity.					✓	✓	✓
Improve maintainability.					✓	✓	✓
Provide scalability.					✓	✓	✓

～ The Stand-Alone Single Channel application pattern

The Stand-Alone Single Channel application pattern provides a structure for applications that have no current need for integration with other systems and need only focus on one delivery channel. While this Application pattern can be used to implement any one of the delivery channels, in this chapter, the focus is primarily on the Web channel.

Business and IT drivers

Table 7.3 summarizes the business and IT drivers for the Stand-Alone Single Channel application pattern.

Table 7.3: *Business and IT drivers for the Stand-Alone Single Channel application pattern*

Business drivers		IT drivers	
Decrease the time to market.	✓	Minimize the application's complexity.	✓
Improve the organizational efficiency.		Minimize the TCO.	
Reduce the latency of business events.		Leverage existing skills.	
Enable easy adaptation during mergers and acquisitions.		Leverage the legacy investment.	
Integrate across multiple delivery channels.		Provide back-end application integration.	
Provide a unified customer view across LOB.		Minimize the enterprise's complexity.	
Support effective cross-selling.		Improve maintainability.	
Support mass customization.		Provide scalability.	

Decreasing the time to market is often the primary business driver for choosing this Application pattern. This approach can be used to extend quickly beyond Web publishing into providing self-service capabilities on the Web.

There should be no immediate business requirements for integrating with back-end applications such as accounting systems, human resources management systems, and insurance-industry policy-processing systems. (These back-end applications might be batch or interactive.) Although Web applications typically do need to integrate with back-end applications, such integration could be postponed until a later stage to improve the time to market and minimize application complexity. Instead, manual processes could be used to synchronize the data between the Web and back-end applications.

This is the ideal Application pattern to choose if the current focus is only on supporting a single delivery channel. In other words, use this pattern if there is no current need for seamless integration between various delivery channels such as Web, voice recognition units, kiosks, and call center applications.

Solution

This is the simplest of all the Application patterns that automate the Self-Service business pattern. As shown in Figure 7.2, the application is divided into two logical tiers. (A tier is a logical layer within a design that allows the subdivision of the application into major functional collections. Tiers can be further subdivided into functional components.)

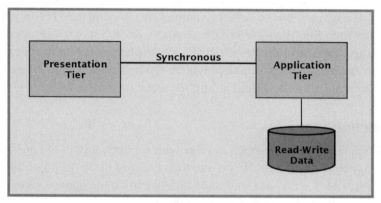

Figure 7.2: The Stand-Alone Single Channel application pattern is relatively simple.

Also, the presentation logic is separated from the business logic. The primary reasons for this separation are to ensure the maintainability of the developed application and to support thin clients. The presentation tier is responsible for all the user-interface-related logic, including data formatting and screen navigation. The application tier is responsible for implementing business logic and accessing data from a local database.

The requester interaction [1] between the presentation tier and application tier is synchronous, which means that any request coming from the user interface directly invokes business logic on the application tier. After the execution of the business logic, control is passed back to the presentation tier, which uses the results to update the user interface.

During the next level of elaboration, these tiers may be further subdivided into more granular functional components. For example, the presentation tier may be partitioned into pieces for user affinity and process affinity. In a typical Web implementation, the user affinity piece can represent the presentation logic that runs the user interface on the client device (in this case, a browser that requests services from a Web server). An example of this is when the JavaScript [2] that implements screen navigation and simple input validation gets downloaded and run on the browser client.

The process affinity piece may represent the dynamic-page-creation aspect of the presentation logic that runs on the server [3]. For example, Java Server Pages (JSP) [4] executed on the server dynamically generate the HTML pages. Web application servers, like IBM's WebSphere Application Servers, are often used to implement this Application pattern. (IBM's WebSphere Application Servers provide an e-business application deployment environment based on open standards. More information can be found at http://www.ibm.com/software/webservers/appserv/.)

Guidelines for use

Some application server vendors can support only the Stand-Alone Single Channel application pattern. If you anticipate a need in the future to integrate your Web applications with back-end applications, you must choose an application server that provides a clear path for such enhancements.

Also, some application server vendors do not promote a clear separation of presentation logic and business logic. If you choose such a vendor, you will increase the total cost of ownership, since lack of clear separation reduces the maintainability of the application. When presentation and business logic are mingled, any changes to the presentation logic can affect the business logic, and vice versa. This results in a significant rewrite of the application.

Separation is especially important in e-business applications, where the user experience and the look and feel of the site need to be constantly enhanced to leverage emerging technologies and to attract and retain site users. New business functions have to be constantly added to the site to meet customer demands and to avoid losing customers to competition. This separation also allows for quick adoption of new types of user interfaces, such as the emerging wireless PDAs and Net appliances. (For further guidelines on multiple device support, refer to Chapter 11.)

Benefits

The Stand-Alone Single Channel application pattern has the following benefits:

- It is the ideal target architecture for applications that have no current or future need for back-end application integration.

- It uses thin clients such as browser-based HTML clients, where the majority of the presentation and business logic runs on the server. The application can be scaled either by increasing the power of the server machine or by spreading the application logic across many servers. This achieves scalability without having to change the Application pattern.

- It uses a connectionless protocol such as HTTP for communication between the user interface clients (browsers) and pieces of the presentation tier run on the server. The server-side component of the presentation tier may maintain a limited number of connections to the application tier (which contains the business logic and accesses the database), and pool these connections across multiple users.

This strategy enables Web applications to scale to support tens of thousands of concurrently active users. In contrast, traditional client/server implementations use protocols that maintain a connection between the user interface clients and servers for every user. Maintaining these connections consumes significant resources on the server. Moreover, there is usually a limit to the maximum number of connections a server can maintain at a time. As a result, traditional client/server applications face severe scalability constraints in supporting thousands of concurrent users. This Application pattern overcomes this scalability problem.

Limitations

The Stand-Alone Single Channel application pattern has the following limitations:

- Since there is no back-end application integration, the Web applications and related data are isolated from other enterprise systems. If many departments in the organization implement such disparate systems, each system might have different data. Synchronizing this information manually is prone to errors and will reduce the overall organizational efficiency. As a result, the total cost of ownership will increase.

- When many departments implement and run disparate Stand-Alone Single Channel applications in an organization, systems management efforts could be duplicated.

- When many Stand-Alone Single Channel applications are run in one organization, business logic reuse could also be a challenge. As a result, the total cost of ownership increases.

- Since this Application pattern does not support integration across various channels (such as the Web, call center applications, and kiosks), users might get different answers from different channels.

Putting the pattern to use

A major insurance company wishes to extend its reach through a Web sales channel. Its existing infrastructure includes a telephone sales channel, and back-end systems (for policies, claims, and billing) that run in batch. It uses "green screen" terminals for online transactions. In the short term, it is not feasible to modify the back-end applications to make them available on a 24/7 basis.

The insurance company chooses to establish an online presence by providing services that do not require back-end integration. These services include locating the nearest office, locating brokers and agents, and using financial calculators and insurance needs-analysis tools. To support this, the insurance firm chooses the Stand-Alone Single Channel application pattern because this pattern does not require back-end integration.

∿ The Directly Integrated Single Channel application pattern

The Directly Integrated Single Channel application pattern provides a structure for applications that need one or more point-to-point connections with back-end applications, but only need to focus on one delivery channel. This Application pattern can also be used to implement any one of the delivery channels, but the focus in this chapter is primarily on the Web channel.

Business and IT drivers

Table 7.4 summarizes the business and IT drivers for the Directly Integrated Single Channel application pattern.

Table 7.4: *Business and IT drivers for the Directly Integrated Single Channel application pattern*

Business drivers		IT drivers	
Decrease the time to market.		Minimize the application's complexity.	
Improve the organizational efficiency.	✓	Minimize the TCO.	
Reduce the latency of business events.	✓	Leverage existing skills.	✓
Enable easy adaptation during mergers and acquisitions.		Leverage the legacy investment.	✓
Integrate across multiple delivery channels.		Provide back-end application integration.	✓
Provide a unified customer view across LOB.		Minimize the enterprise's complexity.	
Support effective cross-selling.		Improve maintainability.	
Support mass customization.		Provide scalability.	

The primary business driver for choosing this Application pattern is to reduce the latency of business events by providing real-time access to back-end applications and data from Web applications. The IT drivers for choosing this Application pattern are to leverage legacy investments and existing skills.

Solution

This Application pattern, shown in Figure 7.3, extends the Stand-Alone Single Channel application pattern by using point-to-point connections to back-end applications and databases.

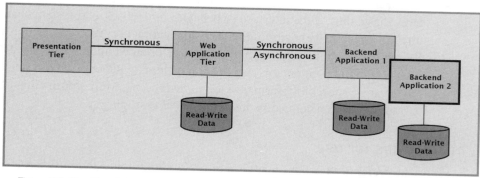

Figure 7.3: The Directly Integrated Single Channel application pattern adds point-to-point connections to back-end applications and databases.

In this pattern, the application is divided into at least three different logical tiers:

- The presentation tier is responsible for all the presentation logic of the application.

- The Web application tier is responsible for implementing some of the business logic and for accessing back-end application logic and data. Usually, new data, such as user profiling information, is put on this tier.

- The back-end application tier may represent a new application, a modified existing application, or an unmodified existing application. The data of existing systems is kept on this tier, and is probably accessible only through the existing back-end application. It is important to note that multiple back-end applications can be accessed by the same Web application tier.

Data can reside on the second and/or the third tier. The requester interaction between the first and second tier is synchronous. The requester interaction between the Web application tier and the back-end application tier can be either synchronous or asynchronous. The chosen requester interaction style between these tiers depends on the characteristics and capabilities of the back-end system. (Bear in mind that a synchronous, or blocking, request at the Application pattern level can be carried over either a synchronous or an asynchronous communications protocol at the Runtime pattern level.)

When integrating with an existing batch system, the requester interaction has to be asynchronous. Integration with back-end transactional systems and database systems, however, can be synchronous. Once again, such connections are direct, without an intermediary; thus, if the interface or behavior of the back-end system changes, it will directly affect the behavior of the Web application tier. Web application servers like WebSphere Application Server and message-oriented middleware like MQSeries are often used to implement this Application pattern. (MQSeries provides heterogeneous any-to-any connectivity from desktop to mainframe. More information can be found at http://www.ibm.com/software/ts/mqseries/messaging/.)

Guidelines for use

The guidelines for the separation of presentation logic and business logic in the Stand-Alone Single Channel application pattern apply here, as well. In addition, the following apply:

- In this Application pattern, corporate data can reside in more than one tier and be distributed physically. As a result, systems management complexity can increase. Hence, care must be taken to ensure that the deployment of this application minimizes such systems management complexities.

- Normally, different IT organizations are responsible for developing the Web applications and maintaining the back-end applications. Under such a scenario, development might be difficult to coordinate, especially if the interfaces between the Web and the back-end application are not properly defined and documented. Hence, it is important to clearly define such interfaces in advance.

Benefits

In addition to providing all the benefits of the Stand-Alone Single Channel, this Application pattern offers the following:

- It works with applications that have simple integration requirements with only a few back-end applications.

- By avoiding manual synchronization of data between back-end applications and the Web application, this pattern overcomes the related shortcomings of the Stand Alone Single Channel application pattern. It increases the organizational efficiency and reduces the latency of business events by providing real-time access to business data and business logic.

- Direct access to back-end applications reduces the duplication of business logic across multiple tiers. As a result, changes to business logic can be made in one tier rather than in multiple applications.

Limitations

The Directly Integrated Single Channel application pattern has the following limitations:

- It focuses on a single channel. Since there is no integration between various delivery channels, users might get different answers from different channels.

- Direct, point-to-point interfaces between the Web applications and back-end applications make this pattern inflexible, especially when there is a need for accessing multiple back-end applications from multiple Web applications. As a result, changes to one application can have knock-on effects on other applications. Under such circumstances, consider more advanced Application patterns such as the Router, Decomposition or Agent, and exploit a hub-and-spoke architecture between the second and third tiers.

Putting the pattern to use

A major insurance company wishes to extend its reach to a Web sales channel. Its existing infrastructure includes a telephone sales channel, and back-end systems (for policies, claims, and billing) that run in batch. The quoting engine, however, can run either online or in batch. The engine uses "green screen" terminals for on-line transactions.

This company has already established an online presence by providing services that do not require back-end integration. These services include locating the nearest office, broker, or agent, and using financial calculators and insurance needs analysis tools. It used the Stand-Alone Single Channel application pattern to achieve a quick implementation of this.

Now the insurance company has realized that manually synchronizing the broker database on the Web application tier with the back-end database is both inefficient and expensive, especially since the company recruits many new brokers every month. In addition, this company wants to provide online quoting services on the Web. Since the underlying quoting rules are complex, the company decides not to duplicate this business logic in multiple tiers.

To meet these requirements, the company chooses to extend the existing applications using the Directly Integrated Single Channel application pattern. It will use an asynchronous batched update to replace the manual update between the Web application tier and the back-end broker database. For the quoting requirements, the company chooses to use a synchronous requester interaction between the Web application and the back-end-quoting engine.

The As-Is Host application pattern

The As-Is Host application pattern provides wider intranet access to existing host applications. These applications might previously have only been available to employees with green-screen devices or PCs with emulators.

Business and IT Drivers

Table 7.5 summarizes the business and IT drivers for this pattern.

Table 7.5: *Business and IT drivers for the As-Is Host application pattern*

Business drivers		IT drivers	
Decrease the time to market.	✓	Minimize the application's complexity.	
Improve the organizational efficiency.	✓	Minimize the TCO.	✓
Reduce the latency of business events.		Leverage existing skills.	✓
Enable easy adaptation during mergers and acquisitions.		Leverage the legacy investment.	✓
Integrate across multiple delivery channels.		Provide back-end application integration.	✓
Provide a unified customer view across LOB.		Minimize the enterprise's complexity.	
Support effective cross-selling.		Improve maintainability.	
Support mass customization.		Provide scalability.	

Time to market is often the primary business driver for choosing this pattern. This approach can be used to quickly implement a green-screen replacement policy so that users can be offered additional browser-based services. The primary IT driver for this Application pattern is to minimize the total cost of ownership by providing browser-based access to existing green-screen back-end applications without rewriting or re-engineering them. This reduces the software distribution cost by eliminating the need for distributing host terminal emulators for 3270/5250/ASCII devices.

Solution

As shown in Figure 7.4, this Application pattern has two logical tiers:

- The empty presentation tier shown in Figure 7.4 represents an off-the-shelf middleware component such as WebSphere Host on Demand, which can be used to provide browser-based access to host applications. (More information about WebSphere Host On Demand can be found at http://www.ibm.com/software/webservers/hostondemand/.)

  The browser-based user interface can be based either on Java applets [5] or HTML. This tier does not include any custom-built code.

- The host application tier represents the existing back-end application.

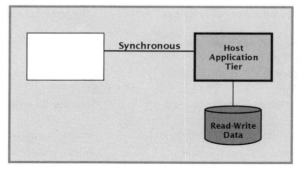

Figure 7.4: The As-Is Host application pattern has two logical tiers.

When this Application pattern is used, the existing back-end application remains as-is. Even though the delivery mechanism is browser-based, the presentation continues to look and behave the same as existing green screens. It uses a synchronous requester interaction between the presentation tier and the existing back-end application tier. Both presentation and business logic continue to run inside the existing host application.

Guidelines for use

Green-screen application usage requires a significant amount of training. Consequently, this presentation style is normally suited for employees (as opposed to external users) and should only be chosen for deploying green-screen applications through an intranet to these users. In some special cases, this strategy can be used to deploy green-screen applications to external users such as business partners.

Benefits

The main benefit of this pattern is that there is no need to modify or re-engineer existing applications; hence, the deployment risk is minimal.

Limitations

Under this scenario, the user interface continues to look and function the same as the existing green-screen interface. Hence, the main limitation of this pattern is that the presentation does not take advantage of the user-friendly features of the browser interface.

Putting the pattern to use

An airline company uses green-screen applications on 3270 terminals for ticketing, check-in, and check-out procedures. The company is quite satisfied with the application as it is and has no current plans to change the user interface. However, it would like to move away from 3270 terminals in order to provide e-mail and Internet access to its employees using a network computer.

Under this scenario, the company can choose to deploy the existing 3270 green-screen applications on network computer terminals or desktop PCs using the As-Is Host application pattern. In doing so, it could choose products such as IBM Host On-Demand.

The Customized Presentation to Host application pattern

The Customized Presentation to Host application pattern can be used to provide a more user-friendly interface to existing host applications without changing the underlying application.

Business and IT drivers

Table 7.6 summarizes the business and IT drivers for this pattern.

Table 7.6: *Business and IT drivers for the Customized Presentation to Host application pattern*

Business drivers		IT drivers	
Decrease the time to market.	✓	Minimize the application's complexity.	✓
Improve the organizational efficiency.	✓	Minimize the TCO.	✓
Reduce the latency of business events.		Leverage existing skills.	✓
Enable easy adaptation during mergers and acquisitions.		Leverage the legacy investment.	✓
Integrate across multiple delivery channels.		Provide back-end application integration.	✓
Provide a unified customer view across LOB.		Minimize the enterprise's complexity.	
Support effective cross-selling.		Improve maintainability.	
Support mass customization.		Provide scalability.	

The primary business driver for choosing this Application pattern is to enhance the usability of existing host applications without rewriting or re-engineering them. These presentation enhancements can take advantage of the user-friendly features provided by graphical user interfaces such as HTML browsers, Java applets, and Java applications. They are preferable to the cumbersome green-screen user interfaces. Such a move not only increases the overall productivity of users of the system, but also reduces the training costs associated with training new users.

The key IT driver is to extend the availability of an existing application to a wider audience without incurring significant application development costs.

Solution

As shown in Figure 7.5, this Application pattern implements a thin client that provides a customized presentation to an existing host application while keeping the back-end system as-is. It has two logical tiers:

- The customized presentation tier accesses the host application and presents the results in a rich GUI format.

- The host application tier represents the existing back-end application.

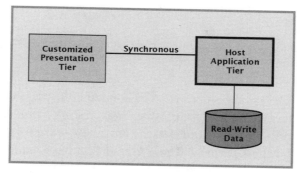

Figure 7.5: The Customized Presentation to Host applica-
tion pattern implements a thin client.

This pattern uses a synchronous requester interaction between the tiers. The client portion of the presentation logic on the browser presents a GUI-rich input screen. This GUI captures the user input and sends it to the server portion of the presentation tier, which converts the GUI input to green-screen input and synchronously communicates with the host application. Subsequently, the results received from the host application are converted to a GUI format and sent to the client for display.

A variation on this Application pattern supports access to the business logic and data on multiple back-end applications so that a combined view can be presented to the user. Middleware products that support this Application pattern include IBM Host Publisher and IBM CICS Gateway for Java.

Guidelines for use

The increased ease of use and universal accessibility of the application through the Web channel can result in more connections than the host can handle. Care must be taken to ensure that the physical implementation does not result in an unsupportable number of connections from the Web. You could, however, increase the capacity of the host application.

Benefits

This approach provides all the benefits of the As-Is Host application pattern, including minimal deployment risk and reduced software distribution cost. In addition, it increases the usability of the system by taking advantage of the user-friendly features provided by GUI interfaces. This ease of use can increase the overall productivity of users and reduce the cost of training new users.

Limitations

The Customized Presentation to Host application pattern has the following limitations:

- The primary focus is on customizing the presentation logic without making any changes to the existing back-end application. Suppose the customized presentation is targeted toward a new set of users, such as customers and business partners. These users might have requirements that cannot be met by the existing back-end application. Hence, the functionality offered by this pattern is limited to the current capabilities of the back-end system.

- There is a tight coupling between the customized presentation logic and host application. As a result, any changes to the host application can require changes to the presentation logic. This increases the maintenance requirements of the system.

- The availability of the Web interface is limited by the availability of the existing host application. The same argument holds true about the performance and scalability of the system. Businesses usually can impose these limitations on internal users of the system, but such limitations cannot be enforced on external users, such as customers and business partners.

Where these limitations apply, you should consider more advanced Application patterns discussed later in this chapter.

Putting the pattern to use

Bank tellers of a regional bank currently use a green-screen CICS application to access account information. Training new users to use this system takes a long time. The bank faces a huge turnover of teller employees and incurs huge initial systems-training costs. To reduce this training cost and increase the productivity of new tellers, the bank wants to develop a user-friendly GUI interface to the accounts management system.

To meet this goal, the bank chooses the Customized Presentation to Host application pattern. The back-end applications already perform very well, so there is no need to rewrite or re-engineer the host system. Under this scenario, the bank uses IBM's CICS Gateway for Java product and deploys a Java-applet-based GUI.

Alternatively, if access to back-end applications other than CICS were required, the bank could have deployed the IBM Host Publisher.

The Router application pattern

The Router application pattern provides a structure for applications that require the intelligent routing of requests from multiple delivery channels to one of multiple back-end applications.

Business and IT drivers

Table 7.7 summarizes the business and IT drivers for this pattern.

Table 7.7: *Business and IT drivers for the Router application pattern*

Business drivers		IT drivers	
Decrease the time to market.		Minimize the application's complexity.	
Improve the organizational efficiency.		Minimize the TCO.	✓
Reduce the latency of business events.	✓	Leverage existing skills.	✓
Enable easy adaptation during mergers and acquisitions.	✓	Leverage the legacy investment.	✓
Integrate across multiple delivery channels.	✓	Provide back-end application integration.	✓
Provide a unified customer view across LOB.		Minimize the enterprise's complexity.	✓
Support effective cross-selling.		Improve maintainability.	✓
Support mass customization.		Provide scalability.	✓

The primary business driver for choosing this Application pattern is to support seamless integration across multiple delivery channels. In the digital economy, users demand universal access to information. To satisfy this demand, many corporations support multiple delivery channels including the Internet, voice recognition units, kiosks, and call center applications.

Users expect to retrieve the same information irrespective of the delivery channel used to access that information. For example, it is important for a discount brokerage firm to ensure that users can retrieve their trade-execution status consistently either through a Web site or through a voice recognition unit. At the same time, these organizations have multiple back-end applications. For example, due to different tax requirements, discount brokerage firms often maintain IRA and regular investment accounts on different back-end applications. Hence, many channels need to access the information from multiple back-end applications.

Applications over a period of time evolve either to take advantage of new technological breakthroughs or to accommodate a changing business environment. Ideally, such changes to one application should be isolated from another. In other words, if a back-end application is replaced with a new system to take advantage of new technology, that replacement should not result in significant changes to all the delivery channels accessing that back-end application. At the same time, a business decision to support a new delivery channel such as wireless PDAs should not require major changes to back-end applications. Such extensibility is especially important for organizations in highly volatile business environments that have plans for mergers and acquisitions. The Router application pattern is ideally suited for such organizations.

The primary IT driver for choosing this Application pattern is to minimize enterprise-wide complexity and reduce the total cost of ownership by using a hub-and-spoke architecture instead of a point-to-point architecture between delivery channels and back-end applications.

Solution

This pattern, shown in Figure 7.6, divides the application into at least three logical tiers:

- The presentation tiers of this Application pattern, unlike the Application patterns discussed so far in this chapter, can support many different presentation styles, including the Internet, call centers, kiosks, and voice recognition units.

- The router tier receives requests from multiple presentation components and intelligently routes them to the appropriate back-end transactions. In doing so, this tier might use a read-only database to look up routing rules. In addition, the router might be responsible for message transformation, protocol conversion, the management of different levels of security, and session concentration. In most cases, the router tier implements minimal business logic. This routing capability can also be used for routing requests from one of the back-end systems to the other.

- The majority of the business logic is concentrated in the back-end application tier.

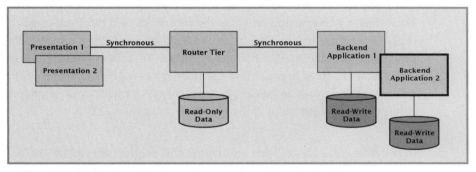

Figure 7.6: The Router application pattern has at least three logical tiers.

A router providing protocol conversion can isolate the back-end transactions from the details of delivery-channel-specific protocols. For example, the Internet application would typically use HTTP for communication between the browser and the server-side portion of the presentation tier, which in turn may use RMI (Remote Method Invocation) [6] or IIOP (Internet Inter-ORB Protocol) [7] to communicate with the router. In contrast, call center applications may use RMI or IIOP to send requests directly to the router. The router tier converts these protocol-specific requests into protocol-independent requests before invoking the back-end transactions. This approach enables you to support new types of delivery channels, such as wireless PDAs, without making any changes to the back-end applications. (More information about RMI can be found at http://java.sun.com/marketing/collateral/javarmi.html.)

Different delivery channels require different levels of security. For example, call-center application users are usually allowed to see certain details about customer accounts that are not shown to customers accessing their accounts through the self-service Web channel. These different levels of security are tightly coupled with the requirements of the delivery channel. Hence, the back-end application should be isolated from these details. The router tier is ideally suited for making such security decisions.

To achieve high scalability and superior performance, session management and session concentration can be done on the router tier. The router tier is thus responsible for establishing a few back-end connections and pooling them for thousands of users originating from multiple delivery channels, when the back-end systems security capabilities permit it.

The requester interaction between the presentation and router tier is synchronous. The requester interaction between the router tier and the back-end application tier is also synchronous. As a result, if the back-end system is unavailable, the business function supported by that back-end application is also unavailable across all delivery channels. (Bear in mind that a synchronous (or blocking) request at the Application pattern level can be carried over either a synchronous or an asynchronous communications protocol at the Runtime pattern level.)

In providing the capabilities outlined in this section, this Application pattern uses elements of the Access Integration and Application Integration patterns (described in Chapters 11 and 12, respectively). For example, in supporting multiple delivery channels, this Application pattern could use the Device Support services observed in Chapter 11. Similarly, the Router tier uses the integration techniques documented in the Application Integration::Router application pattern in Chapter 12.

Web application servers like WebSphere Application Server and message brokers like MQSeries Integrator [8] are often used to implement this Application pattern. (More information about MQSeries Integrator can be found at http://www.ibm.com/software/ts/mqseries/integrator/.)

Guidelines for use

The availability, scalability, and performance observed by the delivery channels are heavily dependent on the availability, scalability, and performance of the back-end applications. Hence, we recommend using robust transaction-processing systems to implement the back-end applications. This pattern can be used to Web-enable either existing or new transaction-processing systems.

While developing new back-end applications or changing existing ones, it is recommended that transactions be defined to be channel-independent and reusable. This will make it easier to extend such transactions to newer channels quickly.

Benefits

This Application pattern offers the following benefits:

- By using routers to manage session concentration and robust transaction processing systems for implementing business logic, it delivers high scalability and superior performance. This is often the target architecture of current high-volume e-business sites.

- The back-end implementation details are isolated from the delivery channels, and the delivery channel implementation details are isolated from the back-end applications. This loosely coupled architecture makes it easy to change, replace, or add back-end applications and delivery channels without heavily affecting other applications in the architecture.

- This loosely coupled architecture also increases maintainability and reduces the total cost of ownership.

- The same back-end transactions are used in this pattern across multiple delivery channels, avoiding duplication of the same business logic on multiple systems. As a result, changes to business logic can be made in one system. This increases the maintainability of the overall system.

Limitations

This Application pattern has the following limitations:

- The availability of certain business functions is heavily dependent on the availability of the back-end applications. Currently, many organizations have transaction processing systems that are only available for a limited amount of time every day. During the rest of the time, they are brought down for batch processing, backup, and maintenance activities. Such systems will have to be enhanced to be available 24/7 to support delivery channels offering Self-Service capabilities on the Web. These enhancements to existing systems can be expensive and time-consuming.

- The focus is primarily on providing access to back-end applications from multiple delivery channels. Most back-end applications are product-specific, and the Router application pattern does not address how to move beyond a product-specific view to a holistic, customer-centric view. Under such circumstances, consider more advanced Application patterns such as the Decomposition and Agent application patterns discussed later in this chapter.

Putting the pattern to use

A premier financial services company currently provides brokerage, mutual fund, banking, and credit card services to its customers. Obviously, these lines of business activities are very different, and they are supported by different back-end applications. Delivery channels operated by the company include Internet self-service, kiosks, voice recognition units, 24-hour call centers, and tellers at the branch offices.

All account information cannot be obtained from all channels. For example, the brokerage and mutual fund accounts can be accessed only through the Internet, voice recognition units, and call centers. On the other hand, the bank account information can be accessed only through kiosks (ATMs), voice recognition units, and tellers at the branch offices.

Currently, different channels use point-to-point connections with back-end applications. Some of them also duplicate the data, which results in inconsistency of information across different channels. Fortunately, most of the product-related back-end applications are robust transaction-processing systems that can be made available on a 24/7 basis.

The company wants to provide consistent access to all product information through all channels. In addition, the target architecture must be highly scalable and highly available, and support superior response time. To achieve these goals, the company chooses the Router application pattern

The Decomposition application pattern

The Decomposition application pattern extends the hub-and-spoke architecture provided by the Router application pattern. It decomposes a single compound request from a client into several simpler requests and intelligently routes them to multiple back-end application. Typically, the responses from these multiple back-end applications are recomposed into a single response and sent back to the client.

Business and IT drivers

Table 7.8 summarizes the business and IT drivers for this pattern.

Table 7.8: *Business and IT drivers for the Decomposition application pattern*

Business drivers		IT drivers	
Decrease the time to market.		Minimize the application's complexity.	
Improve the organizational efficiency.	✓	Minimize the TCO.	✓
Reduce the latency of business events.	✓	Leverage existing skills.	✓
Enable easy adaptation during mergers and acquisitions.	✓	Leverage the legacy investment.	✓
Integrate across multiple delivery channels.	✓	Provide back-end application integration.	✓
Provide a unified customer view across LOB.	✓	Minimize the enterprise's complexity.	✓
Support effective cross-selling.		Improve maintainability.	✓
Support mass customization.		Provide scalability.	✓

All business and IT drivers listed under the Router pattern apply to this Application pattern as well. Additional drivers are described below.

Many organizations have back-end applications that are focused on certain product lines. For example, insurance companies use different systems for supporting health insurance policies and life insurance policies. Such product-specific silos evolved out of necessity, since the business logic and data requirements of different products were vastly different. For this reason, many companies plan to continue to use separate systems for separate product lines.

These same companies, however, want to provide a unified customer view when customers visit the self-service Web sites or contact the call centers, rather than providing a fragmented product-specific view. Similarly, when changes are made to customer information in one system, they should be automatically reflected in other systems. In the example of an insurance company that sells health insurance and life insurance policies, changes to address information should be automatically reflected in both the systems. Such features are increasingly important, since customers often ask for a consolidated view of their multiple accounts.

Solution

This Application pattern, shown in Figure 7.7, is divided into three logical tiers:

- The presentation tier is the same as for the Router application pattern.

- The decomposition tier supports most of the services provided by the router tier in the Router application pattern, including intelligent routing of requests, protocol conversion, security, and session concentration. In addition, it implements the intelligence to break down a single request received from a presentation client into several simpler requests, which it routes to multiple back-end applications. In doing so, it typically uses a local Work In Progress (WIP) database to store routing, decomposition, and recomposition rules and to cache the results from multiple back-end applications until the desired recomposed response has been generated. The decomposition tier implements significantly more business logic than a router tier. Such business logic focuses on providing a unified customer-centric view.

- The majority of the product- and function-specific business logic is still concentrated in the back-end application tier. Some of these back-end applications are highly available and scalable online transaction-processing systems, while others are batch applications.

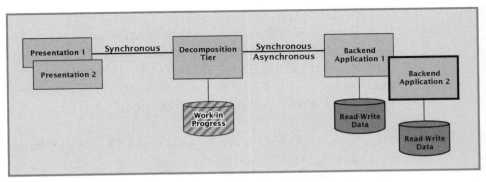

Figure 7.7: The Decomposition application pattern has three logical tiers.

The requester interaction between the presentation and decomposition tier is synchronous. The requester interaction between the decomposition tier and the back-end application tier can be either synchronous or asynchronous.

A synchronous requester interaction is required when the presentation client expects an immediate answer, as in the case with the insurance company and its clients. A customer logs on to the insurance company's self-service Web site and asks to view a consolidated bill. This request is decomposed into multiple synchronous requests that are targeted toward multiple product-specific billing systems. The decomposition tier waits for responses from these systems, combines the results, and displays a consolidated billing view to the customer.

An asynchronous requester interaction between the decomposition tier and back-end applications is appropriate when the presentation client does not expect an immediate response. For example, consider the customer who initiates an electronic transfer of funds to pay for his or her monthly bills using a self-service Web site. This request can be decomposed into two separate requests. The first request is targeted toward a confirmation engine that synchronously provides a confirmation number to the customer for tracking purposes. At the same time, an asynchronous request can be sent to a batch system that transmits an electronic-funds-transfer request to a local bank using EDI technology.

A variation on this pattern includes caching on the second logical tier to avoid a high volume of accesses to the back-end application. Another variation is to use fast asynchronous communications, so that multiple parallel requests can be sent to the third tier to improve response times over serial requests.

As with the Self-Service::Router application pattern, this pattern uses elements of both the Access Integration and Application Integration patterns outlined in Chapters 11 and 12, respectively. In particular, this Application pattern uses the techniques documented in the Application Integration::Broker application pattern in Chapter 12.

As this book goes to press, advanced Web application servers such as WebSphere Enterprise Extensions are planned to enable this Application pattern. A forthcoming release of WebSphere Application Server, Advanced Edition is also expected to integrate with the full range of message-oriented middleware to enable this Application pattern.

Guidelines for use

All the guidelines documented under the Router application pattern apply here as well.

Benefits

This Application pattern provides all the benefits of the Router. In addition, it provides the following:

- A holistic, customer-centric view of information provides an alternative to a fragmented, product-centric view.

- Executing transactions in batch mode, when appropriate, provides several benefits, including the ability to free up systems resources for more important tasks at hand. The Decomposition application pattern enables you to distinguish those transactions and use asynchronous mode for communication with them. This is particularly true for updates that need not be reflected into the appropriate data stores immediately.

Limitations

The focus of this pattern is on providing a consolidated customer-centric view of the information. However, such information is only gathered whenever required and is discarded at the end of the transaction. Hence, this Application pattern does not accumulate all the necessary information in an Operational Data Store (ODS)[9] that can be used for cross-selling and for mass customization of services. Under such circumstances, consider the more advanced Agent application pattern.

Putting the pattern to use

The premier financial services company considered in the discussion of the Router application pattern wants to extend beyond providing consistent access to all product information through all delivery channels. The company wants to provide a consolidated, customer-centric view through all their channels, rather than providing fragmented, product-specific views. For example, they want their customers to see a consolidated net worth across their brokerage, mutual fund, banking, and credit card accounts. Customers should be able to do so through all delivery channels, including Internet self-service, kiosks, voice recognition units, 24-hour call centers, and tellers at the branch offices. To achieve these goals, the company chooses the Decomposition application pattern.

The Agent application pattern

The Agent application pattern structures an application design to provide a unified customer-centric view that can be exploited for mass customization of services, and for cross-selling purposes.

Business and IT drivers

Table 7.9 summarizes the business and IT drivers for this pattern.

Table 7.9: *Business and IT drivers for the Agent application pattern*

Business drivers		IT drivers	
Decrease the time to market.		Minimize the application's complexity.	
Improve the organizational efficiency.	✓	Minimize the TCO.	✓
Reduce the latency of business events.	✓	Leverage existing skills.	✓
Enable easy adaptation during mergers and acquisitions.	✓	Leverage the legacy investment.	✓
Integrate across multiple delivery channels.	✓	Provide back-end application integration.	✓
Provide a unified customer view across LOB.	✓	Minimize the enterprise's complexity.	✓
Support effective cross-selling.	✓	Improve maintainability.	✓
Support mass customization.	✓	Provide scalability.	✓

All the business and IT drivers listed under the Decomposition application pattern apply to this Application pattern as well. In addition, it allows an organization to exploit a unified customer view for mass customization and for cross-selling purposes on an Internet self-service site.

As an example of these requirements, consider a telecommunications company that provides various services, including local telephone access, long-distance services, wireless services, and Internet access. To effectively cross-sell to customers, this company requires a consolidated view of all its relationships with each customer.

Solution

This Application pattern, shown in Figure 7.8, is divided into three logical tiers:

- Refer to the Router application pattern for descriptions of the presentation tier and the back-end application tier.

- The agent tier supports all the services provided by the decomposition tier in the previous Application pattern. It also dynamically builds a consolidated view of the user's relationship with the organization. It uses this to identify ways of mass customizing the organization's goods and services to fit the individual user. This results in "pushing" an additional browser instance in front of the user so he or she can accept or reject the customized offer before continuing with the original task.

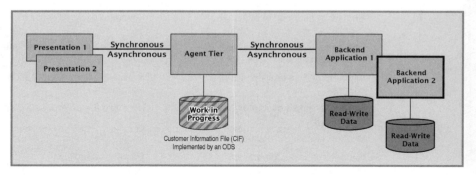

Figure 7.8: The Agent application pattern has three logical tiers.

In a variation on this design, because it is too slow or too expensive to dynamically gather the consolidated view, the organization might choose to implement an Operational Data Store (ODS) that maintains a consolidated Customer Information File (CIF). This CIF provides a current or near-real-time integrated view of all the services subscribed by a customer, aggregated from multiple operational systems. In addition, it stores additional demographic information about customers that has been collected through various sources. This information is used by the Customer Relationship Management (CRM) systems to enhance customer service.

Internet self-service sites can use specialized information to target certain services that match customer demographics. Call center applications can use this demographic information to prompt customer service representatives (CSR) with cross-selling scripts to solicit customers to subscribe to additional services. This cross-selling process can also be driven programmatically by an application (expert system) drawing conclusions from the customer data. Another variation on this design allows the Work In Progress database held by the agent tier to also be used to hold long-running transaction data before committing such information to back-end applications.

Consider a mortgage-company Web site that allows customers to submit a detailed application for a home mortgage online. Users of this site can complete their loan applications over several log-in sessions. In other words, the site allows customers to save their "work in progress" loan applications and complete them later. Such an application is not submitted to the back-end loan approval engine until the customer has completed the entire application. The agent tier can be effectively used to store such long-running transactions before committing a completed transaction to the back-end application.

The majority of the product- and function-specific business logic is still concentrated in back-end applications. Some of these back-end applications are highly available and scalable online transaction-processing systems, while others are batch applications.

The requester interaction between all the tiers can be either synchronous or asynchronous. This asynchronism across tiers means that with an appropriate application design, the overall availability of the system is not affected by the unavailability of one of the systems. In other words, if one back-end application is not available, the presentation tier should still be able to receive requests targeted toward that back-end application and store such requests to be processed later, when the application becomes available.

In providing these capabilities, this Application pattern uses elements of both the Access Integration and Application Integration patterns outlined in Chapters 11 and 12, respectively. Specifically, it may use the Application Integration::Broker and Data-Focused Application Integration::Operational Data Store techniques documented in Chapter 12.

Guidelines for use

All the guidelines listed under Decomposition apply to this Application pattern as well. In addition, because of possible data inconsistencies between back-end applications, it might be preferable to reconcile the data first, using the ODS variation described above. The accuracy of the insights drawn about a customer's likes and dislikes depends heavily on the quality of the CIF operational data store and the algorithms used for interpreting this data.

Creating such a CIF operational data store is both time-consuming and complex. Once the data store has been created, it needs to be kept up to date by synchronizing the information between the unified customer-centric view and the product-centric application data. In addition, demographic information has to be purchased from external sources on a regular basis and synchronized with the CRM operational data store. Care must be taken to clearly design business processes and technical infrastructure to create, update, and enhance the CIF operational data store.

Benefits

The Agent application pattern provides all the benefits of the Decomposition application pattern. In addition, it enables mass customization of products and services provided by an enterprise to a market of one, by using personalization techniques. Similar techniques are used for effective cross-selling.

Limitations

By using a hub-and-spoke architecture, the Agent application pattern aims to minimize the complexity of meeting all the business and IT drivers. In spite of this attempt, the implementation of this pattern is complex, especially since the implementation of an ODS is often complicated, and involves synchronization of information between the CIF and back-end operational systems.

At this time, there are few off-the-shelf middleware products that can provide the end-to-end functionality required by this Application pattern.

Putting the pattern to use

A telecommunications company currently provides various services, including local telephone access, long distance services, wireless services, and Internet access. The company has built this impressive portfolio of services primarily through mergers and acquisitions. As a result, the company has inherited a number of product-specific back-end applications.

To keep up with the ever-changing landscape of technology and to quickly capture market share in new areas such as wireless Internet access, telephony over Internet Protocol (IP), and broadband Internet access through cable, the company plans to continue to aggressively seek acquisition and merger partners. These trends suggest that more and more product-specific systems will be acquired in the future.

The overall success of this company's aggressive growth strategy depends on its ability to effectively cross-sell different services to all its customers. When customers call the call center to pay their bills, CSRs should be able to effectively solicit them to subscribe to additional services. Such solicitation must be done not only based on a customer's current subscription level, but also on the demographics of the customer. Similarly, when customers log onto their Internet accounts, the welcome page must be personalized to reflect their interests.

To achieve the stated goals and cope with the continued existence of multiple product-specific back-end applications, the company chooses to implement the Agent application pattern. It chooses to build a CIF operational data store that provides a consolidated customer-centric view. The agent tier will use this data for sophisticated personalization and cross-selling purposes.

Step 6a: Identify Application patterns in the FECS solution

Step 3 of the case study, discussed in Chapter 4, identified the existence of two Self-Service business patterns within the FECS solution. The first occurrence of the Self-Service business pattern was observed where customers perform product selection, order entry, and inventory checking. The second instance was observed where customers register and enter their preferences into the system.

A more detailed look at the technical requirements for the product-selection and inventory-checking functions reveal the following:

- The user is online, so these functions need to be synchronous in nature. In other words, the user will be waiting for an immediate response to the action he or she initiated during the session

- The Web-based functions need to integrate with an existing inventory-control system that cannot be modified to support the new functions.

From a business perspective, the chosen architecture should be able to support multiple delivery channels in the future. From an IT perspective, the integration between the Web application tier and the back-end application tier should reduce the enterprise-wide complexity and minimize the total cost of ownership. This can be achieved by a hub-and-spoke architecture instead of using point-to-point integration between the Web applications and the back-end applications.

Based on these requirements, the solution will need to have the following components:

- The clients will need the ability to operate in a network connected mode.

- The application tier in this pattern should be able to:

  - Support two-way communication with clients.

  - Route messages to the back-end systems in a format that can be understood by these systems.

  - Wait for a response back from the back-end system and translate the message into a format that can be understood by the client.

  - If the back-end system does not respond, ensure that the server times out and handles the error condition appropriately.

Matching these requirements to the business and IT drivers of the various Application patterns for Self-Service indicates that the Self-Service::Router application pattern would be required to automate this Business pattern.

A more detailed look at the technical requirements for the customer registration function reveals the following:

- The user is online, so the registration function needs to be synchronous in nature. In other words, the user will be waiting for an immediate response to the action initiated during the session.

- A user can use the registration function to access, change, and remove information related to his or her profile from the directory that supports the FECS solution.

Based on these requirements, the solution will need to have the following components:

- The clients will need the ability to operate in a network connected mode.
- The application tier in this solution should be able to:
  - Support two-way synchronous communication with clients.
  - Be a able to read and write data into a directory.

These requirements can be implemented using the Self-Service::Stand Alone Single Channel application pattern, shown in Figure 7.9.

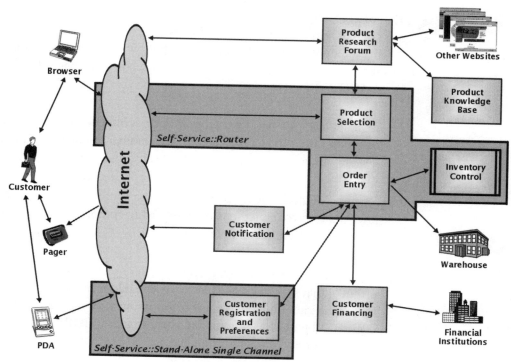

Figure 7.9: The FECS solution uses two Self-Service application patterns.

References

[1] Requester interaction—Describes the style of requester interaction between one tier and another.

[2] JavaScript—An interpreted programming or script language. Interpreted languages generally take longer to process than compiled languages, but are very useful for shorter programs.

[3] Server—A program that awaits and fulfills requests from client programs in the client/server model. A given application may function as a client with requests for services from programs, and also as a server of requests from other programs.

[4] JSP—Provides a simple yet powerful mechanism for inserting dynamic content into Web pages. The JSP specification achieves this by defining a number of HTML-like tags that allow developers to insert server-side Java logic directly into HTML or XML pages that are sent to HTTP clients.

[5] Java applet—A small Java program that is intended not to be run on its own, but rather to be embedded inside another application. It usually gets downloaded from the server and runs inside the browser.

[6] Remote Method Invocation (RMI)—A protocol that enables a Java program to invoke methods on another Java program that can be located on a different computer.

[7] Internet Inter-ORB Protocol (IIOP)—An object-oriented programming protocol that makes it possible for distributed programs written in different programming languages to communicate over the Internet. IIOP is a critical part of a strategic industry standard, CORBA (Common Object Request Broker Architecture).

[8] MQSeries Integrator—Combines a one-to-many connectivity model, plus transformation, intelligent routing, and information flow modeling. It facilitates the development of new application services that integrate the functions of multiple, disparate existing business systems.

More information can be found at http://www.ibm.com/software/ts/mqseries/integrator/

[9] Operational Data Store (ODS)—A data store containing detailed, partially reconciled, and nearly current data used for immediate informational needs. Users can often write additional data to this form of data store. It is a hybrid between a data warehouse, which is accessed often on a read-only basis, and a transactional data store, which is accessed on a high-volume read-write basis.

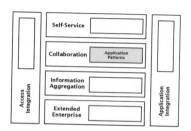

Application patterns for Collaboration

The Collaboration business pattern can be observed in e-business solutions that allow users to communicate and share data and information with other users or groups of users on the network. This Business pattern captures the process of identifying and locating users on the network and facilitating sharing of information between these users. The collaboration can be synchronous, through services such as instant messengers and chat rooms, or asynchronous, through mechanisms such as e-mail and bulletin boards.

The Collaboration business pattern addresses the interactions between individual users or groups of users who may be in the same location or dispersed geographically across the world. This pattern can be observed even in many of the earliest e-business solutions such as e-mail and bulletin boards. In fact, three out of the four building blocks of the TCP/IP protocol (FTP, Telnet, and SMTP) are geared toward fostering collaboration among users, machines, and applications.

Solutions that foster and promote collaboration between users are critical components in today's world of one-to-one marketing and more knowledgeable and powerful consumers. Consider the very popular instant messenger services provided by many online services such as AOL and MSN. These services allow individuals to instantaneously locate and interact with other users who are logged on to the network.

These services allow individuals to set up or be part of groups that are built around some common interest (such as a team working on a particular project) or have some common characteristic (such as members of a family). They also allow individuals to locate other individuals or groups across the globe and collaborate directly with them. The nature of this collaboration could be a simple exchange of textual messages, or it could be a more interactive whiteboard application that allows multiple users to see the same document in real-time and make their changes to it.

The Collaboration business pattern

It is rare to see these collaborations as stand-alone solutions; they usually enhance the features and functions provided by an overall solution. This chapter describes four Application patterns, shown in Figure 8.1, that can be used to represent the functions and interactions supported by the Collaboration business pattern. In addition, this chapter documents criteria by which you might evaluate these Application patterns for adoption in your own projects.

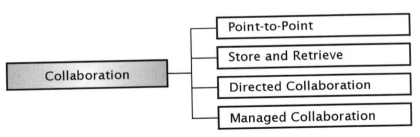

Figure 8.1: These four Application patterns represent the functions and interactions supported by the Collaboration business pattern.

Summary of business and IT drivers for Collaboration

Tables 8.1 and 8.2 summarize the business and IT drivers for each Application pattern described in this chapter.

Table 8.1: *Business drivers for the Collaboration application patterns*

Business drivers	Point-to-Point	Store and Retrieve	Directed Collaboration	Managed Colaboration
Decrease the time to market.	✓	✓	✓	✓
Improve the organizational efficiency.	✓	✓	✓	✓
Reduce the latency of business events.	✓	✓	✓	✓
Enable easy adaptation during mergers and acquisitions.		✓	✓	✓
Require instantaneous collaboration.	✓		✓	✓
Require deferred collaboration.		✓		✓
Require workflow collaboration.				✓
Support many users.		✓	✓	✓

Table 8.2: *IT drivers for the Collaboration application patterns*

IT drivers	Point-to-Point	Store and Retrieve	Directed Collaboration	Managed Collaboration
Leverage existing skills.	✓	✓	✓	✓
Provide network-addressing independence.		✓	✓	✓
Provide managed service.		✓	✓	✓
Improve maintainability.		✓	✓	✓
Support complex data types.			✓	✓
Provide significant network bandwidth.			✓	✓

The Point-to-Point application pattern

The Point-to-Point application pattern allows users to directly address other users on the network using simple point-to-point synchronous communications. It then enables the users to begin a direct communication link. This pattern dictates that each user can establish this synchronous connection to another user by specifying the direct physical address (such as a TCP/IP address or a fully specified machine name) of the other user.

Business and IT drivers

Table 8.3 summarizes the business and IT drivers for this pattern.

Table 8.3: *Business and IT drivers for the Point-to-Point application pattern*

Business drivers		IT drivers	
Decrease the time to market.	✓	Leverage existing skills.	✓
Improve the organizational efficiency.	✓	Provide network-addressing independence.	
Reduce the latency of business events.	✓	Provide managed service.	
Enable easy adaptation during mergers and acquisitions.		Improve maintainability.	
Require instantaneous collaboration.	✓	Support complex data types.	
Require deferred collaboration.		Provide significant network bandwidth.	
Require workflow collaboration.			
Support many users.			

Time to market is often the primary business driver for choosing this Application pattern. This approach can be used to establish collaboration between users of a solution without having to go through the detailed process of establishing and setting up a local/global directory and building in the application code necessary to use this directory.

Since this Application pattern relies on online and instantaneous point-to-point communication, the latency of business events is very low. In fact, with this pattern, a message from a sender can be delivered instantaneously, provided the receiver is online and ready to accept the message.

This is the ideal Application pattern to choose if the current objective is to establish simplistic collaboration functions within an application. This solution is also applicable when there are no additional enhancements needed to these collaboration functions. The solution is also cost-effective to develop. However, these cost savings can be very easily offset by the maintenance or support costs. Also, the overall complexity increases as more users or functions are added to the solution.

This pattern is not a good fit for solutions where users have to collaborate across departmental or organizational boundaries, or where there is very little control of how the other users are set up and configured on the network. However, the decentralized nature of this collaboration pattern makes it an ideal choice for the establishment of instant and temporary networks that do not have a central registry or authority.

Solution

This is the simplest of all Application patterns that automate the Collaboration business pattern. Unlike the structure observed in the Application patterns for other business patterns (such as Self-Service, discussed in Chapter 7), the structures for Collaboration application patterns do not have tiers or any order of hierarchy. As shown in Figure 8.2, the participants in this pattern are as follows:

- The client is a peer to the other clients with which it collaborates. This implies that these clients will have identical capabilities and functions. However, in order to support synchronous communications, these participants should alternate roles between being senders and receivers of information.

- Each client has a local persistent data store used to hold the IP addresses, preferences, and other details that facilitate effective collaboration between users.

The clients used in this Application pattern can detect a network connection with the other client and will be able to establish a new connection where one does not exist. They use a local list of addresses to determine the physical network address (TCP/IP address) of a partner on the network. The clients should also have the intelligence built in to be able to communicate over this network connection using a specific protocol (such as TCP/IP) and be able to decode and encode the messages in the specified protocol.

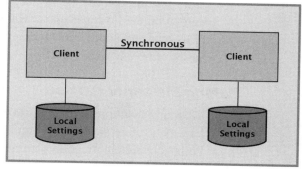

Figure 8.2: Point-to-Point is the simplest Collaboration application pattern.

During the next level of elaboration, the Point-to-Point application pattern can be further defined using more granular functional components. For example, the client may be partitioned into a lookup-and-connect process that is responsible for establishing the network connection, and a Codec (coder/decoder) function that can be used to enable the collaboration functions.

Guidelines for use

This pattern should be used when:

- The overall nature of communications is simple and is synchronous.

- The number of users who use the solution is small.

- The application developer has control over all of the clients that are part of the solution.

- The network addresses are relatively static.

- No other viable option is available for implementing this solution.

Benefits

This Application pattern is very easy to use. It provides a solution in situations where the nature of collaboration (the type of data or the amount of data exchanged) is very specialized and cannot be handled by collaboration solutions that can be purchased in the marketplace.

Limitations

Since most of the application code developed to support this Application pattern is custom-built, the process of maintaining and upgrading the code will be an added burden on the IT department. Maintaining this code requires a good understanding of lower-level application and networking protocols. These skills are typically both hard to find and expensive.

Putting the pattern to use

Most of the solutions that use this Application pattern tend to be custom-coded. However, there are many prominent examples of Web-based solutions that use the Point-to-Point application pattern. The best known among these is Gnutella.

Gnutella, a point-to-point solution for sharing music, is built on a decentralized and temporary network of users with no central point of control. A user who wants to use Gnutella downloads a client program and a host list of users from the Web. This list provides the addresses of a limited number of peers (usually five to 10) with whom the user can collaborate on a regular basis. Users can connect to the network through the client and establish connections with the peers on their lists.

Each peer on the network has a host list of his or her own and can establish connections with other users on the Web. This dynamic and cascading link to peers results in a network of millions of users. All search requests are propagated across the network until the file is located. Once this is done, the user can establish a direct link with the peer who has the file and initiate a file transfer request to download the file to his or her machine.

Other solutions that use the Point-to-Point application pattern include custom-developed programs such as TCP/IP sockets programs, which enable communications between programs and applications. These custom-developed programs typically:

- Should know the address of the collaboration partner in order to open communication channels (a socket) to it

- Will play the role of a sender by posting messages and data to the socket to be sent to the destination, and play a receiver when it is listening to the channel for data

- Can support the transportation of any data stream without having to know about the content of the data stream

There are many commercially available products that in some instances can be used to facilitate the Point-to-Point pattern, such as Microsoft's NetMeeting. Any user who has the NetMeeting client installed can initiate calls to any other user on the network as long as:

- The user knows the address of the other person on the network. This could be the TCP/IP address or a hostname.

- The person on the other end has the NetMeeting client on his or her machine, and it is running and listening for incoming calls.

- The receiver accepts the call.

The Store and Retrieve application pattern

The Store and Retrieve application pattern allows users to collaborate with others on the network interactively. Unlike the Point-to-Point application pattern, this pattern does not require both partners to be online at the same time. It also does not require the client to know the physical or direct address of other users of the solution.

Business and IT drivers

Table 8.4 summarizes the business and IT drivers for this pattern.

Table 8.4: *Business and IT drivers for the Store and Retrieve application pattern*

Business drivers		IT drivers	
Decrease the time to market.	✓	Leverage existing skills.	✓
Improve the organizational efficiency.	✓	Provide network-addressing independence.	✓
Reduce the latency of business events.	✓	Provide managed service.	✓
Enable easy adaptation during mergers and acquisitions.	✓	Improve maintainability.	✓
Require instantaneous collaboration.		Support complex data types.	
Require deferred collaboration.	✓	Provide significant network bandwidth.	
Require workflow collaboration.			
Support many users.	✓		

This approach can be used to very quickly establish collaboration between users of a solution without having to develop a lot of custom code. Since this Application pattern does not require the client to know the physical or direct address of its partners, it is easy to establish collaboration between users in the enterprise and across enterprises.

This is the ideal Application pattern to choose if the current focus is to establish simplistic collaboration functions within a solution. This pattern is also applicable when the clients have intermittent network connections, and it is difficult to predict when the collaboration partner will be connected to the network. A solution using this pattern is also cost-effective to develop.

This pattern is not a good fit where the solution calls for very little latency in communication between the users. It is also not a good fit when the collaboration should include large files or rich media such as streaming audio and video.

Solution

As shown in Figure 8.3, the main participants in the Store and Retrieve application pattern are as follows:

- The client is a peer to the other clients with which it collaborates. The client should be aware of the address of the server to which it needs to connect. To support true synchronous and asynchronous communications, these participants should alternate roles between being senders and receivers of information.

- Each client has a local data store that is used to retain copies of the data the user wants to keep on his or her own machine.

- Each client connects to a server, which authenticates the clients and allows it to log in. Once this is done, the client can store messages for other clients on the server.

- The server has a local data store that is used to hold and save messages, documents, and other media transmitted from clients. When a client logs in, the server notifies the client of content stored on the server for it, and allows the client to pull this content down across the network.

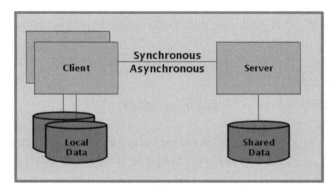

Figure 8.3: This represents the Store and Retrieve application pattern.

Guidelines for use

This pattern should be used when:

- The physical or direct addresses of other clients on the network are not known.

- Both synchronous and asynchronous communication need to be supported. This provides the ability to support a wide range of solutions, from bulletin boards and workrooms to interactive chat rooms.

- Multiple clients will log in and share information with other users by posting messages on (or sending e-mails to) a server for later retrieval.

Benefits

The Store and Retrieve application pattern has the following benefits:

- It is simple to implement.

- Since this pattern does not require that a client know the direct address of the destination, it is ideal for solutions where the network addresses are not published or change frequently.

- Most of the functions of this pattern can be implemented using commercially available collaboration solutions.

- This pattern requires very minimal custom code, and hence is cost-effective to maintain.

Limitations

This pattern has the following limitations:

- It calls for the implementation of server software and associated hardware to support new users. This will add to the overall complexity of the solution.

- The nature and type of collaboration supported by this pattern are simplistic. For more complex communications, consider one of the other Application patterns described in this chapter.

Putting the pattern to use

Both first- and second-generation collaboration solutions use the Store and Retrieve application pattern. One of the most common examples is an e-mail system based on SMTP (Simple Mail Transfer Protocol) and POP (Post Office Protocol). Any user who wishes to use the e-mail system will have to be registered with the e-mail server. Consider a Hotmail user. To send an e-mail message to another, this user will:

- Start up the e-mail client (such as the mail client that is a part of Netscape Navigator or Microsoft Outlook Express).

- Create a new e-mail message and address the message to the second user (or groups of users).

- Select the option to send the e-mail message.

The e-mail client connects to the mail server and sends the message to the server, which in turn directs the message to the inbox of the other user, who may be another Hotmail user or any other e-mail user who has access to the Internet. It will also check to see if there are any messages waiting in the current user's inbox. If there are, it will download these messages for processing on the client machine. The e-mail message sent by the user will be delivered to the recipient when he or she logs in to the server.

The Store and Retrieve application pattern can also be observed in bulletin boards, chat rooms based on Internet Relay Chat (IRC) protocol, and Lotus Teamrooms.

～ The Directed Collaboration application pattern

The Directed Collaboration application pattern allows users to collaborate with others on the network interactively. This pattern requires that the two users who need to interact are online simultaneously. It also requires users to register with a server. In this pattern, all of the users are peers; there are no client-server or master-slave relationships between the tiers in the pattern.

Business and IT drivers

Table 8.5 summarizes the business and IT drivers for this pattern.

Table 8.5: *Business and IT drivers for the Directed Collaboration application pattern*

Business drivers		IT drivers	
Decrease the time to market.	✓	Leverage existing skills.	✓
Improve the organizational efficiency.	✓	Provide network-addressing independence.	✓
Reduce the latency of business events.	✓	Provide managed service.	✓
Enable easy adaptation during mergers and acquisitions.	✓	Improve maintainability.	✓
Require instantaneous collaboration.	✓	Support complex data types.	✓
Require deferred collaboration.		Provide significant network bandwidth.	✓
Require workflow collaboration.			
Support many users.	✓		

This approach can be used to quickly establish collaboration between users of a solution without having to develop a lot of custom code. It allows users to simultaneously and interactively modify shared applications and data.

This pattern requires all the users to register with the server. The user's profile, preferences, and security privileges are stored on a server directory, so the client does not need to know the physical or direct address of other clients. It also lets you implement different security levels, and implement more complex collaboration styles that include sharing applications and complex data types.

This is the ideal Application pattern to choose if the current focus is to establish synchronous, sophisticated collaboration functions within a solution. This solution is also applicable when the clients have permanent and preferably high-speed network connections. The solution is also cost-effective to develop because many of these functions are available in off-the-shelf products. However, this pattern is not a good fit for solutions where there are limitations on the processing power of the clients.

Solution

As shown in Figure 8.4, the main participants in the pattern are as follows:

- The client is a peer to other clients with which it collaborates.

- Each client has a local address book where the user can set up the users that he or she will communicate with regularly. The user can also set up groups of users and collaborate with them collectively. The local address book also stores the address of the server to which it connects when initiating collaboration functions.

- The clients could optionally contain software programs (such as word processors and spreadsheet programs) that can be shared across the network.

- This Application pattern requires that each client register with the server. Once a client has registered, the user's data and profile are stored in a directory on the server. When the client connects to the server, the server authenticates the user by validating his or her access privileges against the directory. The server will notify the user of others who are currently online, and return the network addresses of those clients. The client can then use this information to initiate direct collaboration with the other clients. In other words, the client uses the server for authorization, authentication, and directory lookup.

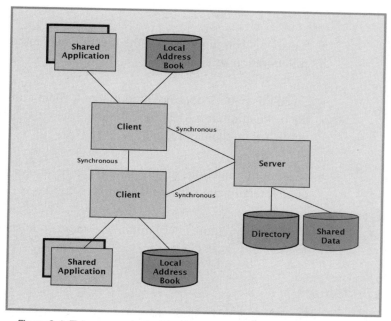

Figure 8.4: This represents the Directed Collaboration application pattern.

Guidelines for use

This pattern should be used when:

- The user does not know the physical or direct addresses of other clients on the network.

- All the registered users might not be online at the same time.

- There is a requirement for sharing simple and complex applications and data types.

- A server can be set up that will allow multiple clients to log in and share information with other users in an online and synchronous manner.

Benefits

The Directed Collaboration application pattern has the following benefits:

- It supports complex collaboration styles.

- It also lets you implement authentication and authorization for the individual collaboration sessions.

- Since this pattern does not require that a client know the direct address of the destination, it is ideal for solutions where the network addresses are not published or change frequently.

- Most of the functions of this pattern can be implemented using commercially available collaboration solutions.

- This pattern requires very minimal custom code, and hence is cost-effective to maintain.

Limitations

This pattern calls for the implementation of server software and associated hardware to support new users. This will add to the overall complexity of the solution.

Putting the pattern to use

One of the most popular applications on the Web is the Instant messenger service provided by AOL, ICQ, and Lotus's Sametime. These applications use the Directed Collaboration application pattern to implement instant and online collaboration. Each of these applications has a global directory where users can register and specify their preferences. These applications also require a custom client program that will connect to a server to facilitate the collaboration process with other users.

Lotus's Sametime and Microsoft's NetMeeting provide a more sophisticated form of collaboration. These products support the basic chat and collaboration functions, but they also provide other functions, such as the following:

- Sharing documents and applications. For instance, during an active collaboration session, a user can share a Microsoft Word document with other users. These users can view and interactively change the data in the document, as long as they have the Microsoft Word software running on their individual machines.

- Sharing rich media. The chat session can support sharing audio and video data, in addition to simple chat.

One of the most popular and controversial Web sites on the Internet in recent times is Napster, whose architecture is based on the Directed Collaboration application pattern. In Napster, all users are registered at the server. A user logs in, is authenticated, and publishes a set of files to share on the server. The user can also search the server's store for other files that may be of interest. Once the user finds a file, he or she can select a peer to download it from. The Napster client then establishes a point-to-point communication with the other Napster user to request and download the file.

The Managed Collaboration application pattern

The Managed Collaboration application pattern builds on the Directed Collaboration application pattern by implementing workflow rules to manage the collaboration between users of the solution. This pattern supports both synchronous and asynchronous collaboration.

Business and IT drivers

Table 8.6 summarizes the business and IT drivers for this pattern.

Table 8.6: *Business and IT drivers for the Managed Collaboration application pattern*

Business drivers		IT drivers	
Decrease the time to market.	✓	Leverage existing skills.	✓
Improve the organizational efficiency.	✓	Provide network-addressing independence.	✓
Reduce the latency of business events.	✓	Provide managed service.	✓
Enable easy adaptation during mergers and acquisitions.	✓	Improve maintainability.	✓
Require instantaneous collaboration.	✓	Support complex data types.	✓
Require deferred collaboration.	✓	Provide significant network bandwidth.	✓
Require workflow collaboration.	✓		
Support many users.	✓		

This pattern provides all of the benefits provided by the Directed Collaboration application pattern. In addition, this pattern helps implement a managed, step-by-step collaboration process. These capabilities are very important when there is a requirement for several solutions that include but are not limited to:

- Applications that support collaborative and incremental development of business functions, supporting distributed project teams

- Applications where the collaboration is driven by specific conditions or preferences

- Applications that support collaborations driven by the content of the messages, such as a customer service solution which directs a customer to a specific customer service representative who is familiar with a specific product or service

Solution

As shown in Figure 8.5, the structure of the Managed Collaboration application pattern is very similar to the Directed Collaboration pattern, extending it with a few more components:

- The clients in this pattern have a temporary data store that they use to store local data. This allows these clients to work on a local copy of the data before it is replicated to the shared data repository on the server.

- The servers in this pattern can connect into a workflow application that provides the capability to move data from one user/process to another based on predefined rules stored in a rules database. These rules can include:

  - Simple flows that marshal the data through a predefined workflow consisting of a fixed sequence of steps

  - Directed flows that establish the destination of the data based on where or who the message originated from

  - Dynamic flows that establish the destination of the data based on the content of the message

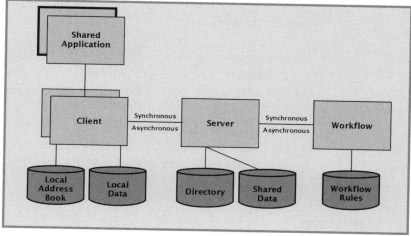

Figure 8.5: This represents the Managed Collaboration application pattern.

Guidelines for use

This pattern should be used when:

- The physical or direct addresses of other clients on the network are not known.

- All of the users might not be online at the same time.

- There is a requirement for sharing simple and complex applications and data types.

- A server can be set up that will allow multiple clients to log in and share information with other users in an online and synchronous manner.

Benefits

The Managed Collaboration application pattern has the following benefits:

- It supports complex collaboration styles.

- It lets you implement authentication and authorization on the individual collaboration sessions.

- Since this pattern does not require that a client know the direct address of the destination, it is ideal for solutions where you do not know the network addresses, or where these addresses change frequently.

- This Application pattern lets you implement automated techniques such as e-mail filtering and targeted marketing communications, which are key for implementing sophisticated Customer Relationship Management solutions on the Web.

Limitations

This pattern has the following limitations:

- The workflow processes require custom coding and the definition of workflow rules. However, most of the workflow-related functions are available in commercially available workflow engines.

- This pattern calls for the implementation of server software and associated hardware to support new users. This will add to the overall complexity of the solution.

Putting the pattern to use

Most commercial and customer-focused Web sites have an area that allows customers, investors, and others to provide feedback to the organization. These sites also allow users to ask specific questions about their products and services. From the customer's viewpoint, the Web site is a single point of contact into the organization. However, within the organization, questions related to products might go to the manufacturing department, questions related to service might go to customer service, and feedback on products and services might go to the quality control department. These solutions can use the Managed Collaboration application pattern to implement the feedback functions and set up dynamic workflows that could include looking for selected keywords in incoming messages and routing them to appropriate destinations.

Computational resource sharing applications are another class of solutions that use the Managed Collaboration application pattern. In this type of solution, clients participate in a network and make their resources available for use by other peers on the network. The most common example of such a solution on the Web is the project, which allows anyone with an Internet-connected PC to join the search for extraterrestrial intelligence. While this solution is not part of the Search for Extra-Terrestrial Intelligence (SETI) Institute, it helps analyze data collected from the Arecibo Radio Telescope in Puerto Rico.

The main concept behind the solution is to take advantage of the unused processing cycles of peers on the network by offloading processing and computational tasks to them, as follows:

- An interested computer owner downloads free screen-saver software from SETI@home.

- Once this software is installed on the computer, it senses when the computer is idle (for example, when the user leaves to take a lunch break), and downloads a 300 KB chunk of data for analysis from the central server.

- The results of this analysis are sent back to the server, where they are combined with the crunched data from the many thousands of other participants, and used to help in the search for extraterrestrial signals.

The tremendous advantage of this scheme is that it provides access to unused gigaflops of processing capacity that would otherwise be expensive to procure.

Step 6b: Identify Application patterns in the FECS solution

Step 3 of this process, discussed in Chapter 4, identified the existence of a Collaboration pattern within the FECS solution. A more detailed look at the requirements for the customer notification function of the solution shows that:

- There are two-way communications with the users.

- Users will not always be connected.

- Users are automatically notified when certain events occur within the solution. For instance, an e-mail is sent to the user as soon as his or her order is confirmed by the FECS solution.

Based on these requirements, the solution will need to have the following components:

- The clients will need the ability to operate in both a network-connected and disconnected mode.

- The servers in this pattern should be able to:
  - Support two-way communication with clients.
  - Send messages to clients triggered by dynamic events within the solution.

In other words, there is a need for store and retrieve collaboration. Comparing these requirements against the Business and IT drivers of the various Application patterns in this chapter, it is clear that the Collaboration::Store and Retrieve application pattern would be required. This is shown in Figure 8.6.

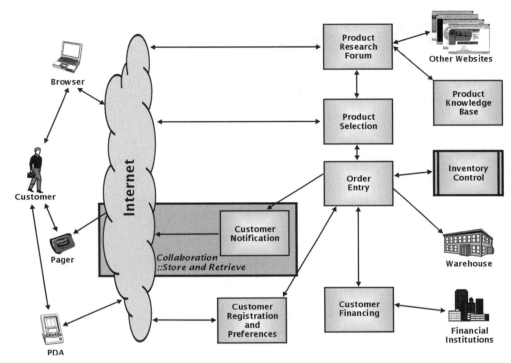

Figure 8.6: The FECS solution uses the Collaboration::Store and Retrieve application pattern.

C H A P T E R

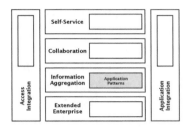

Application patterns for Information Aggregation

The Information Aggregation business pattern can be observed in e-business solutions that allow users to access and manipulate data aggregated from multiple disparate sources. This business pattern captures the process of using tools to extract meaningful information from large volumes of structured data such as purchase orders and transaction histories, or unstructured data such as text, images, and video.

While specific techniques used for aggregating and distilling structured and unstructured data vary, there are two distinct steps involved, as shown in Figure 9.1: Population and Information Access.

Population involves designing and creating applications to extract, cleanse, restructure, and move data into or between appropriate data stores. The arrow in Figure 9.1 represents this step. It is needed if the required data does not already exist in the appropriate data store, or if the data is not in an optimal form to satisfy the user's needs.

Consider a large grocery-store chain. Location managers of its stores would like to receive a daily report summarizing perishable items that

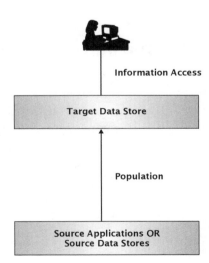

Figure 9.1: The two basic steps in the Information Aggregation business pattern are Population and Information Access.

must be placed on sale to clear the inventory before they expire. Such a Decision Support System (DSS) would need to distill information from a vast inventory data store. Inventory data is most likely not optimally structured to run such reports. A Population application must be developed to extract the relevant data from the inventory management system and structure it in a way that facilitates optimal access. In this scenario, the Population application primarily deals with structured data.

Consider also a financial services portal that aggregates securities analysis from multiple sources and categorizes such information into different folders. In this scenario, the Population step involves crawling the selected Web sites for the specified information, creating an index of selected articles, and then categorizing them. This example identifies the need for a Population step in aggregating and distilling meaningful information from unstructured data.

Information Access involves designing and creating the user interface and processes for unraveling relevant information from raw data to meet the business needs of the user. A solid line in Figure 9.1 represents this step. Information Access applications cover a wide range of functions, from simple queries to complex data mining. Self-Service application patterns (described in Chapter 7) can also serve as front ends of a data store created and maintained by the Population applications described in this chapter, thus providing information access to users.

The Information Aggregation business pattern

The specific business functionality supported by applications that automate the Information Aggregation business pattern vary from one industry to the other. A closer survey of such applications in multiple industries, however, reveals certain common approaches that have been successful. In this chapter, such successful approaches are captured by the Application patterns shown in Figure 9.2.

Designing applications that automate the Information Aggregation business pattern can be challenging for many reasons. User requirements tend to be vague and constantly changing. Several applications might be built simultaneously, some with common data needs and others with conflicting needs.

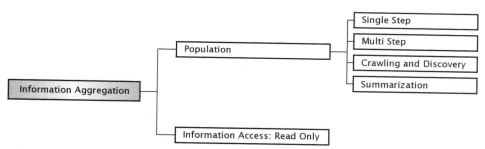

Figure 9.2: The Application patterns shown here are the focus of this chapter.

To overcome these challenges, best practice suggests that Population and Information Access functionality should be separated during design. An end-to-end application that automates the Information Aggregation business pattern can be implemented by combining one or more of the four Population application patterns with the Information Access application pattern. This separation allows for greater flexibility in changing either the Population function or the Information Access function without affecting the other, thus promoting component reuse.

Summary of business and IT drivers for Information Aggregation

Tables 9.1 and 9.2 summarize the IT and business drivers for each Application pattern described in this chapter.

Table 9.1: *IT drivers for the Information Aggregation application patterns*

IT drivers	Population – Single Step	Population – Multi Step	Population – Crawling and Discovery	Population – Summarization	Information Access – Read Only
Minimize total cost of ownership (TCO).	✓	✓	✓	✓	✓
Promote consistency of operational data.	✓	✓			✓
Improve maintainability.	✓	✓	✓	✓	✓

Table 9.2: *Business drivers for the Information Aggregation application patterns*

Business drivers	Population – Single Step	Population – Multi Step	Population – Crawling and Discovery	Population – Summarization	Information Access – Read Only
Improve the organizational efficiency.	✓	✓	✓	✓	✓
Reduce the latency of business events.	✓	✓	✓	✓	✓
Distill meaningful information from vast amount of structured data	✓	✓			
Extensive reconciliation, transformation, and restructuring of structured data.		✓			
Provide easier access to vast amount of unstructured data through indexing and categorization.			✓	✓	
Enhance access to unstructured data through summarization.				✓	
Provide access to distilled information and drill-through capability.					✓

～ The Population–Single Step application pattern

The Population–Single Step application pattern structures the population of a data store with data that requires minimal transformation and restructuring.

Business and IT drivers

Table 9.3 summarizes the business and IT drivers for this pattern.

The primary business driver for choosing the Population–Single Step application pattern is to copy data from the source data store to a target data store with minimal transformation. The main reason for copying the data is to avoid manipulating the primary source of a company's operational data, which is often maintained by operational systems.[1]

Business drivers		IT drivers	
Table 9.3: *Business and IT drivers for the Population–Single Step application pattern*			
Improve the organizational efficiency.	✓	Minimize total cost of ownership (TCO).	✓
Reduce the latency of business events.	✓	Promote consistency of operational data.	✓
Distill meaningful information from vast amount of structured data.	✓	Improve maintainability.	✓
Extensive reconciliation, transformation, and restructuring of structured data.			
Provide easier access to vast amount of unstructured data through indexing and categorization.			
Enhance access to unstructured data through summarization.			
Provide access to distilled information and drill-through capability.			

Solution

The Application pattern shown in Figure 9.3 represents the basic data population functionality with a "read dataset…process…write dataset" model. One or more source data stores can be read by the Population application. These source data stores are created and maintained by other processes. The target data store is the output from the Population application. These can be the final output from the process, or they can be temporary data stores used as the source for another step in the process.

The metadata contains the rules describing which records from the source are read, how they are modified (if needed) on their way to the target, and how they are applied to

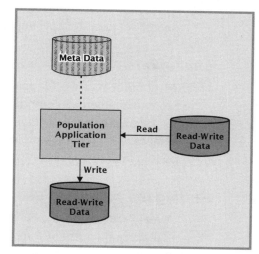

Figure 9.3: This represents the Population–Single Step application pattern.

the target. The rules are depicted in this way to emphasize the best practice of having a rules-driven application, rather than hard-coding the rules in the application, to facilitate maintenance. This logical dataset also holds a variety of metadata describing the output that the Population application produces, such as statistics and timing information.

In general, both the source and the target can contain any type of data, including structured and unstructured data. However, in most cases, this Application pattern is used for propagating structured data from one data store to another.

In providing the capabilities outlined above, this Application pattern uses common services related to data-focused integration, such as data replication, cleansing, transformation, and augmentation. These common services are further elaborated in Chapter 12.

Guidelines for use

It is highly recommended that the logic governing the transformation of source data into target data be implemented using rules-driven metadata, rather than be hard-coded. This approach enhances the maintainability of the application and hence reduces the total cost of ownership.

Benefits

This is the ideal architecture when the required transformation between the source and target data store is simplistic.

Limitations

Most of the real-world requirements for propagating structured data from one data store to another are complicated, requiring extensive reconciliation, transformation, restructuring, and merging of data from multiple sources. Under such circumstances, consider the more advanced Population–Multi Step application pattern discussed later in this chapter.

Putting the pattern to use

A real estate company wants to distribute individual sales summaries to all its realtors in the form of a spreadsheet on a periodic basis. Such a sales summary should provide a breakdown based on the location of the property and the month of sale of the property. The sales summary would be extracted periodically from a database maintained by the real-time property listing system used for recording business transactions. Since the objective is to produce simple derived data from simple source data with minimal transformation, the real estate company implements the Population–Single Step application pattern.

~ The Population–Multi Step application pattern

The Population–Multi Step application pattern structures the population of a data store with structured data that requires extensive reconciliation, transformation, and restructuring.

Business and IT drivers

Table 9.4 summarizes the business and IT drivers for this pattern.

Table 9.4: *Business and IT drivers for the Population–Multi Step application pattern*

Business drivers		IT drivers	
Improve the organizational efficiency.	✓	Minimize total cost of ownership (TCO).	✓
Reduce the latency of business events.	✓	Promote consistency of operational data.	✓
Distill meaningful information from vast amount of structured data.	✓	Improve maintainability.	✓
Extensive reconciliation, transformation, and restructuring of structured data.	✓		
Provide easier access to vast amount of unstructured data through indexing and categorization.			
Enhance access to unstructured data through summarization.			
Provide access to distilled information and drill-through capability.			

The primary business driver for choosing this pattern is to reconcile data from multiple data sources and to transform and restructure it extensively to enable efficient access to information. This pattern is best suited for the aggregation and distillation of meaningful information from structured data.

Solution

In this Application pattern, the building block provided by the Population–Single Step pattern is repeated several times to achieve the desired results. The intermediate target data created in one step acts as the source data for the next step. Figure 9.4 depicts the common three-step process. The application is divided into three logical tiers: extract, transform, and load. In most best-practice implementations, these functional steps contain additional subtasks.

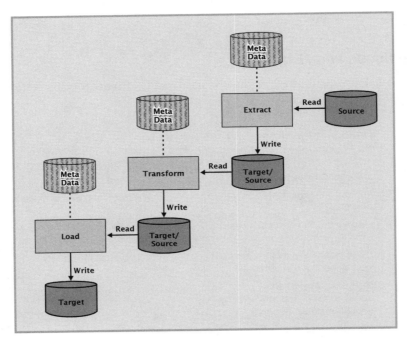

Figure 9.4: This represents the Population–Multi Step application pattern.

The extract tier extracts data from the source data store. This data store is typically owned by another application and used in a read/write fashion by that application. The extraction rules may range from as simple as including all data, to a more complex rule, prescribing the extraction of only specific fields from specific records under varying conditions.

The transform tier transforms data from an input to an output structure according to the supplied rules. Transformation covers a wide variety of activities, including reconciling data from many inputs, validating and cleansing data of errors, and transforming data in individual fields based on predefined rules or based on the content of other fields. When two or more inputs are involved, there is generally no guarantee that all inputs will be present when required. The transform step must be able to handle this situation.

The load tier loads the input data into the target data store. As with the extract tier, the load tier can range from a simple process of overwriting the target data store to a complex process of inserting new records and updating existing records.

The actual implementation can involve fewer or more steps. In such cases, the diagram in Figure 9.4 must be adjusted accordingly, and consideration must be given to the placement of any additional tiers.

It is also important to note that this Application pattern has been generalized to cover any source and target data stores. However, the details of the population process operate differently depending on the type of source and target data stores and their relationship. For example, the details of populating a data mart [2] from a Business Data Warehouse (BDW) [3] would be different from the details of populating an Operational Data Store (ODS) from an operational system. The details of these various population scenarios are outside the scope of this book. For more information, refer to the "Patterns for e-business" Web site or *Data Warehouse—From Architecture to Implementation* by Barry Devlin (Addison-Wesley, 1997).

Like the Population–Single Step pattern, this Application pattern uses elements of Application Integration in providing the capabilities outlined above. In particular, it uses common services related to data-focused integration such as data replication, cleansing, transformation, and augmentation described in Chapter 12.

Guidelines for use

It is highly recommended that the logic governing the extraction, transformation, and loading of data be implemented using rules-driven metadata, rather than be hard-coded. As mentioned for the previous pattern, this approach enhances the maintainability of the application.

Benefits

This is the ideal architecture when the complex transformation of structured data between the source and target data store is required.

Limitations

Reconciling data from multiple sources is often a complex undertaking and requires a considerable amount of effort, time, and resources. This is especially true when different systems use different semantics.

Putting the pattern to use

Consider a financial services company that provides various services, including checking account, savings account, brokerage account, and insurance. The company has built this impressive portfolio of services primarily through mergers and acquisitions. As a result, the company has inherited a number of product-specific operational systems.

The company would like to create a Business Data Warehouse that provides a consolidated view of customer information. It would like to use this consolidated information for sophisticated pattern analysis and fraud detection. Populating such a BDW would require reconciling customer records from different operational systems that use different identification mechanisms to identify the same customer. Further, each operational system records the transaction with different time dependencies. The reconciliation process must resolve these semantic and time differences, as well as check for any inconsistencies and irregularities. Due to the complexity involved, the financial services company chooses the Population–Multi Step application pattern.

~ The Population–Crawling and Discovery application pattern

The Population–Crawling and Discovery application pattern provides a structure for applications that retrieve and parse documents, and creates an index of relevant documents that match the specified selection criteria.

Business and IT drivers

Table 9.5 summarizes the business and IT drivers for this pattern.

Table 9.5: *Business and IT drivers for the Population–Crawling and Discovery application pattern*

Business drivers		IT drivers	
Improve the organizational efficiency.	✓	Minimize total cost of ownership (TCO).	✓
Reduce the latency of business events.	✓	Promote consistency of operational data.	
Distill meaningful information from vast amount of structured data.		Improve maintainability.	✓
Extensive reconciliation, transformation, and restructuring of structured data.			
Provide easier access to vast amount of unstructured data through indexing and categorization.	✓		
Enhance access to unstructured data through summarization.			
Provide access to distilled information and drill-through capability.			

The primary business driver for choosing this pattern is to select relevant documents from a vast collection, based on specified selection criteria. The objective is to provide quick access to useful information instead of bombarding the user with too much information.

Search engines that crawl the Web implement this Application pattern. It is best suited for selecting useful information from a huge collection of unstructured text data. A variation of this pattern can be used for working with other forms of unstructured data, such as image, audio, and video files.

Solution

This Application pattern, shown in Figure 9.5, for the most part follows the framework of the Population–Single Step application pattern. In this case, however, the crawl-and-discover tier crawls from one data store to the next, retrieving documents, parsing them, and building an index of those that match the selection criteria.

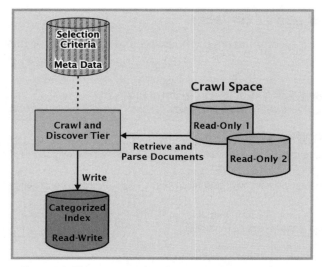

Figure 9.5: This represents the Population–Crawling and Discovery application pattern.

In some cases, the selected links may be grouped into predefined categories. In other cases, similar links may be joined, resulting in a federated index where a single index entry may point you to more than one document.

Web search engines often use links within a retrieved document as the next set of data stores to crawl. As a result, these search engines discover new documents that otherwise would have been unknown to the application. This true dynamic nature is the key distinguishing factor between the earlier Population application patterns and this one.

Guidelines for use

There are several packaged crawl-and-discover products available to implement this Application pattern. When evaluating such products, place a high weight on the ability to accept flexible selection criteria. This would enable wider usage of the product.

Benefits

This is the ideal architecture for extracting useful information from a vast set of un-structured data.

Limitations

This Application pattern merely creates an index entry with a link to the original document. It does not provide a summary of the content found in these documents. Hence, users will need to drill through each document to determine its usefulness. This could be inefficient and time-consuming. Under such conditions, consider the more advanced Population–Summarization application pattern described later in this chapter.

Putting the pattern to use

Consider a large software company with a huge array of products. It develops vast amounts of technical documentation to support these products. Each product line publishes its own documentation on its own departmental Web site. As products change, so does the documentation. Locating a particular piece of information in this sea of ever-changing data can be quite challenging and time-consuming.

To improve the efficiency of information access, the company wants to create a categorized and federated index of all the documents. Such an index must be refreshed periodically to keep it current. To meet these requirements, the software company chooses to implement the Population–Crawling and Discovery application pattern.

The Population–Summarization application pattern

The Population–Summarization application pattern extends the capabilities provided by the previous pattern by attaching summary information to index entries.

Business and IT drivers

Table 9.6 summarizes the business and IT drivers for this pattern.

All the business and IT drivers listed under Population–Crawling and Discovery application pattern apply to this pattern as well. In addition, the company wants to attach a brief summary to index entries describing the content of each linked document.

Table 9.6: *Business and IT drivers for the Population–Summarization application pattern*

Business drivers		IT drivers	
Improve the organizational efficiency.	✓	Minimize total cost of ownership (TCO).	✓
Reduce the latency of business events.	✓	Promote consistency of operational data.	
Distill meaningful information from vast amount of structured data.		Improve maintainability.	✓
Extensive reconciliation, transformation, and restructuring of structured data.			
Provide easier access to vast amount of unstructured data through indexing and categorization.	✓		
Enhance access to unstructured data through summarization.	✓		
Provide access to distilled information and drill-through capability.			

Solution

This Application pattern, shown in Figure 9.6, adds summarization capability to the previous one. It is easier to attach a summary to index entries if selected documents contain a summary that is clearly marked. This is often the case with Web sites that are professionally developed. However, when a summary does not already exist, extracting one electronically is quite tricky and often imprecise.

Guidelines for use

It is important to establish a company-wide guideline requiring all documents published on the Web to include clearly marked summary information. This will enhance the effectiveness of this Application pattern.

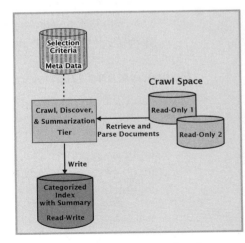

Figure 9.6: This represents the Population–Summarization application pattern.

Benefits

This is the ideal architecture for extracting useful information (including summary descriptions) from a vast set of unstructured data.

Limitations

Search engines often crawl and discover documents on Web sites that are maintained by organizations beyond their influence. This is especially true if the selection criteria require them to crawl the Internet, which is outside the boundaries of the organization. Under such circumstances, some of the selected documents might not have precise summary information attached. Selecting many such documents could undermine the effectiveness of the summarization process.

Putting the pattern to use

Consider the large software company example from the previous Application pattern. If it wants to enhance the effectiveness of its categorized and federated index, it might want to attach summary information to index entries. Under such circumstances, it could choose to implement the Population–Summarization application pattern.

~ The Information Access–Read Only application pattern

The Information Access–Read Only application pattern helps structure a system design that provides read-only access to aggregated information.

Business and IT drivers

The primary business driver for choosing this Application pattern is to provide efficient access to information that has been aggregated from multiple sources. This mechanism can access both structured and unstructured data populated by one or more of the Population application patterns discussed earlier in this chapter. Internal and/or external users may use this information for decision-making purposes.

Table 9.7 summarizes the business and IT drivers for this pattern.

Table 9.7: *Business and IT drivers for the Information Access–Read Only application pattern*

Business drivers		IT drivers	
Improve the organizational efficiency.	✓	Minimize total cost of ownership (TCO).	✓
Reduce the latency of business events.	✓	Promote consistency of operational data.	✓
Distill meaningful information from vast amount of structured data.		Improve maintainability.	✓
Extensive reconciliation, transformation, and restructuring of structured data.			
Provide easier access to vast amount of unstructured data through indexing and categorization.			
Enhance access to unstructured data through summarization.			
Provide access to distilled information and drill-through capability.	✓		

As an example of this driver, an Executive Information System (EIS) [4] might generate a summary report on a periodic basis that compares the sales performance of various divisions of a company with the sales targets of those divisions. This Application pattern is used to access the information from structured raw data. In addition, the application may provide drill-through capability, allowing the user to track the performance of individual sales representatives against their individual targets.

Similarly, this Application pattern can be used for searching the summary and index created by the Population–Summarization application pattern, which retrieves and parses unstructured data such as text from selected Web sites and attaches summary information to the index. Even here, the application can provide drill-through capability, allowing the user to navigate to the complete document for further details.

Solution

In this scenario, as shown by Figure 9.7, the application is divided into at least three logical tiers:

- The presentation tier is responsible for all the user-interface-related logic, including data formatting and screen navigation. In some cases, the presentation could be as simple as a printout.

- The primary application tier is responsible for accessing the associated read-only data store and distilling the required information from this data.

- The drill-through application tier and its associated data store provide the ability to drill through to detailed data. If drill-though capability is not required, this tier is not implemented. For example, data necessary to enable drill-through might already exist and be accessed from an existing information access application or might be defined in the scope of this information access application.

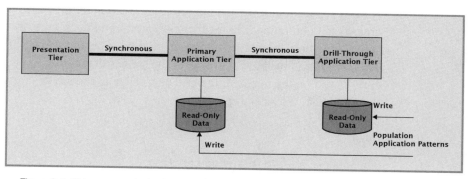

Figure 9.7: This represents the Information Access–Read Only application pattern.

Note the positioning of the data store population, represented by arrows in Figure 9.7. One or more of the Population patterns discussed earlier in this chapter could be used to meet this need. The population of the data store usually occurs independently of the information access.

Users may alter their own copies of the aggregated data. In the majority of cases, such changes are not propagated back to the source application from which the data was extracted. When multiple source applications are involved, propagating changes back to the source can be extremely complex, requiring two-way synchronization of data.

At the outset, you might find architectural similarities between the Information Access application pattern and applications that automate the Self Service business patterns. However, these two are distinguished by the user interaction with data versus a business transaction. The Information Access application pattern facilitates direct interaction between users and data, hence providing significant freedom and flexibility in accessing and manipulating data. Applications that automate the Self-Service business pattern, on the other hand, enable direct interaction between users and business transactions, thus enabling users to electronically perform a business process.

However, as mentioned earlier in this chapter, a few of the Self-Service application patterns can provide front-end data stores created and maintained by the Population applications described in this chapter, thus providing information access.

Guidelines for use

A clear separation of the presentation logic from the information access logic increases the maintainability of the application and decreases the total cost of ownership. This allows the same information to be accessed using various user interfaces. This separation of logic also allows the same information to be packaged differently based on the needs of the end user. Hence, this layered approach decreases the total cost of ownership.

Benefits

This pattern has the following benefits:

- The use of read-only data provides for maximum consistency in a multi-user analysis or reporting environment.

- Its simplicity reduces the implementation risk.

- This simple yet powerful Application pattern meets the majority of the information aggregation and distillation needs.

Limitations

This Application pattern does not propagate changes made to reconciled data back to the source applications. For such integration requirements, the pattern must be customized to implement an Operational Data Store. (For guidelines on implementing Operational Data Stores, refer to Chapter 12.)

Putting the pattern to use

Consider a personal portal such as my.yahoo.com that aggregates information from disparate data sources and allows users to personalize this information to meet their preferences. These portals aggregate both structured data, such as weather information and stock quotes, and unstructured data, such as news and links to other sources of information. Based on the type of data and the amount of transformation required, the portal developers might choose one or more of the Population application patterns discussed in this chapter. Once the data has been stored in the optimal format, the portal developers offer the Information Access–Read Only application pattern so users can access this information in a personalized style, and have drill-through capabilities.

Step 6c: Identify Application patterns in the FECS solution

Step 3 of the case study process, discussed in Chapter 4, identifies the existence of the Information Aggregation business pattern within the FECS solution. A more detailed look at the requirements for the product research forum shows that:

- There is a need to automatically and periodically access relevant public and private Web sites to discover information related to the product.

- There is a need to define specific selection criteria (metadata) that limits the sites searched and the type of information aggregated.

- The results of the search need to be summarized to make the information more useful to the user.

Based on these requirements, the solution will need to have the following capabilities:

- Provide easier access to a vast amount of unstructured data.

- Crawl and discover data from external Web sites on a regular basis.

- Minimize the number of sites crawled by using a specific set of rules.

- Summarize the acquired data and make it available for access from multiple clients.

Since the business and IT drivers of the Information Aggregation::Population–Summarization application pattern clearly match these requirements, this pattern can be used to automate the product research forum functionality. This is shown in Figure 9.8.

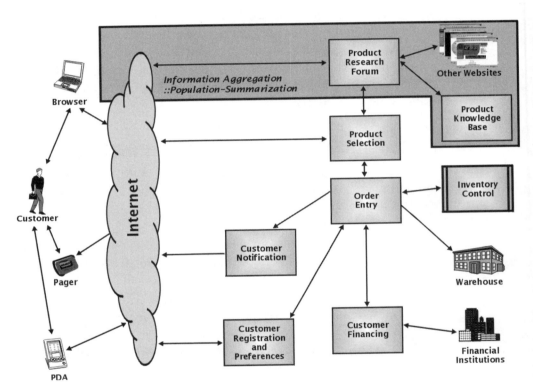

Figure 9.8: The FECS solution incorporates the Information Aggregation application pattern.

References

[1] operational systems—Are often transactional systems that implement a significant business process or task. They can be interactive, as in the case with applications that automate the Self-Service business pattern, or batch, such as legacy mainframe systems that run on a periodic basis.

[2] data mart—A data store defined and designed to meet the information needs of a group of users or a department. It contains the required data, either detailed or summarized, and structured according to the query or reporting needs of the user. Data marts are often used in a read-only fashion and come in a variety of forms, including relational databases, multi-dimensional databases, spreadsheets, and Web marts.

[3] Business Data Warehouse (BDW)—A data store containing detailed, reconciled, and historical data, structured according to an enterprise data model and designed to be the single, consistent source for all management information. This data source is seldom accessed by end-users, and then only in a read-only format.

[4] Executive Information System (EIS)—Provides high-level business information (balanced scorecard figures, key indicators, and so on) to upper management or executives. This information is often delivered to the user as a discrete item of work either automatically or on-demand.

CHAPTER 10

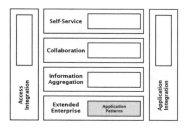

Application patterns for Extended Enterprise

The Extended Enterprise business pattern addresses the interaction of business processes between two distinct organizations. Large, multi-business unit organizations that operate semi-autonomously can also exploit this pattern internally, just as separate organizations do externally.

In particular, this pattern deals with programmatic interfaces between inter-enterprise applications. The golden rule of business-to-business integration is "the less you know about the business partners' non-shared processes and application implementation details, the better off you are." This allows for loose coupling between partner applications that enables organizations to evolve their applications without affecting their business partners' applications. The general problem addressed by these patterns is illustrated in Figure 10.1.

An interaction between partners forms one or more shared processes. These shared processes are referred to as *public processes*. However, these partners need to retain their organizational independence, so

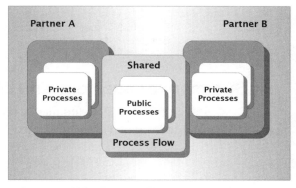

Figure 10.1: The Extended Enterprise business pattern deals with the interactions of private and public processes.

the notion of separation of processes into public and private is required. *Private processes* are not shared and are fully under the control of the individual partner. A private process could be as simple as passing data to a particular application, or as sophisticated as initiating or resuming a multi-step workflow involving several applications and user interactions. This separation of public and private processes provides the benefit of flexibility and autonomy to the trading partner community, especially as the network grows beyond simple exchanges between two partners.

The Extended Enterprise business pattern

The specific business functionality supported by applications that automate the Extended Enterprise business pattern varies from one industry to another. A survey of such applications in multiple industries, however, reveals certain common approaches that have been successful. This chapter captures these successful approaches in the five Application patterns shown in Figure 10.2. In addition, this chapter documents the criteria by which you can evaluate these Application patterns for adoption in your own projects.

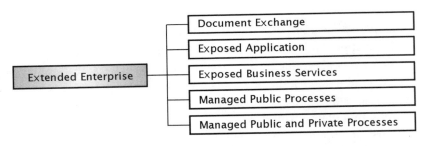

Figure 10.2: These five Application patterns can be used to automate the Extended Enterprise business pattern.

Summary of business and IT drivers for Extended Enterprise

Tables 10.1 and 10.2 summarize the business and IT drivers for each Application pattern described in this chapter.

Table 10.1: *Business drivers for the Extended Enterprise application patterns*

Business drivers	Document Exchange	Exposed Application	Exposed Business Services	Managed Public Processes	Managed Public and Private Processes
Improve the organizational efficiency.	✓	✓	✓	✓	✓
Reduce the latency of business events.	✓	✓	✓	✓	✓
Support a structured exchange with business partners.	✓	✓	✓	✓	✓
Support partner real-time access to/from applications.		✓	✓	✓	✓
Support partner real-time access to/from business services.			✓	✓	✓
Support shared public process flows with partners.				✓	✓
Integrate the internal workflow manager with partner-shared business process flows.					✓

Table 10.2: *IT drivers for the Extended Enterprise application patterns*

IT drivers	Document Exchange	Exposed Application	Exposed Business Services	Managed Public Processes	Managed Public and Private Processes
Leverage existing skills.	✓	✓	✓	✓	✓
Leverage the legacy investment.	✓	✓	✓	✓	✓
Enable back-end application integration.		✓	✓	✓	✓
Minimize application complexity.	✓	✓	✓	✓	✓
Minimize enterprise complexity.			✓	✓	✓
Avoid partner-mandated infrastructures.				✓	✓
Reduce partner dependency on specific applications.			✓	✓	✓
Reduce partner dependency on specific business protocols.				✓	✓

~ The Document Exchange application pattern

The Document Exchange application pattern helps to structure the batched electronic exchange of data using mutually agreed-upon message formats.

Business and IT drivers

Table 10.3 summarizes the business and IT drivers for this pattern.

Table 10.3: *Business and IT drivers for the Document Exchange application pattern*

Business drivers		IT drivers	
Improve the organizational efficiency.	✓	Leverage existing skills.	✓
Reduce the latency of business events.	✓	Leverage the legacy investment.	✓
Support a structured exchange with business partners.	✓	Enable back-end application integration.	
Support partner real-time access to/from applications.		Minimize application complexity.	✓
Support partner real-time access to/from business services.		Minimize enterprise complexity	
Support shared public process flows with partners.		Avoid partner-mandated infrastructures.	
Integrate the internal workflow manager with partner-shared business process flows.		Reduce partner dependency on specific applications.	
		Reduce partner dependency on specific business protocols.	

The primary business driver for choosing this Application pattern is to increase the efficiency of interactions between enterprises. Instead of exchanging paper documents, this Application pattern can be used to send and receive documents electronically. This eliminates the need for the error-prone process of manually re-entering data.

This is the ideal Application pattern to choose if your current business needs would be satisfied by the batched exchange of electronic documents. In other words, it is best if your business requirements don't call for direct invocation of a business partner's systems in a real-time fashion.

Large organizations often require their business partners to exchange messages electronically. For example, they might mandate the use of Electronic Data Interchange (EDI)[1] transaction sets over a particular Value Added Network (VAN) [2] for certain interactions, such as placing an order.

Solution

This Application pattern is divided into at least three different logical tiers:

- The partner tier represents a set of trading-partner applications whose characteristics are unspecified. In other words, the technological implementation details of these systems are not disclosed. However, trading partners mutually agree upon the message format and the means of exchanging these messages.

- The translator tier retrieves the mutually agreed-upon messages from a persistent buffer and decodes them into messages that can be used by the internal business processes of the receiving organization. Decoded messages are then stored in a Work In Progress (WIP) data store.

- The back-end application tier is responsible for processing the decoded messages. In doing so, it typically reads decoded messages directly from the WIP data store.

  Hence, Figure 10.3 shows a direct communication link between the back-end application tier and the data store. After processing decoded messages, back-end applications may, in turn, generate responses to be delivered back to the partner who sent the initial message. In such cases, a reverse flow of messages may be observed.

If a business partner was requested to take part in a request for tender, a series of messages would need to be exchanged as part of this business process. Partner A would have to build custom business logic to link the applications that process these various types of messages, in order to automate the overall business process. In such a case, the private processes clearly get intermingled with the public process—and if the public process should ever change, the whole business logic will need to be redone. Hence, Figure 10.3 shows the private and public processes as a single entity rather than two separate entities.

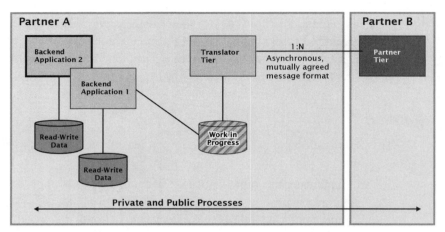

Figure 10.3: The Document Exchange application pattern is divided into at least three logical tiers.

The batched exchange of electronic documents implies asynchronous communication between partners. Hence, there is a need for a persistent buffer that stores all the messages received from multiple partners to be translated and processed later.

This Application pattern is best suited for implementing EDI-based integration over a VAN between organizations. Alternatively, EDI can be used over Web technologies that have emerged recently. In both cases, the translator tier is implemented using EDI translation packages.[3]

Guidelines for use

Choose an EDI translation package that is rules-based so you can map EDI messages to internal messages using rules. This allows the quick definition and redefinition of messages. You might also want to consider more sophisticated translation packages that convert EDI messages into automatic requests to a transaction monitor, such as an order processing system.

Benefits

The electronic exchange of documents increases the efficiency and reduces the latency of business interactions between organizations.

Limitations

As mentioned earlier, this Application pattern is best suited for implementing EDI-based integration between organizations. EDI is a well-established standard, but it is deployed only by a small number of companies. Participation in an EDI-based network requires a subscription to a particular VAN, which is typically expensive. Furthermore, it mandates the use of certain IT infrastructure by all partners. As a result, you lose flexibility in connecting to business partners who might have different IT infrastructure capabilities. This Application pattern, therefore, can be both expensive and inflexible. It focuses on achieving batched exchanges of information and cannot be used for gaining direct access to specific services provided by partner systems.

Consider an online travel agency that needs to confirm a hotel room reservation and provide a confirmation number to the customer in a real-time fashion. Here, the travel agency system might need to interface directly with the reservation system of the hotel chain and execute the required transaction instantaneously. Under such circumstances, consider the more advanced Application patterns discussed later in this chapter.

Putting the pattern to use

An auto parts manufacturer enters into an agreement to supply parts to a major car manufacturer. The car manufacturer manages its supply chain through an established EDI network. It mandates all suppliers to communicate using auto-industry EDI transaction sets. To meet this mandate, the auto parts manufacturer chooses the Document Exchange application pattern.

The Exposed Application application pattern

The Exposed Application application pattern helps to structure a system design that allows specific applications to be directly accessed by partner systems across organizational boundaries.

Business and IT drivers

Table 10.4 summarizes the business and IT drivers for this pattern.

Table 10.4: *Business and IT drivers for the Exposed Application application pattern*

Business drivers		IT drivers	
Improve the organizational efficiency.	✓	Leverage existing skills.	✓
Reduce the latency of business events.	✓	Leverage the legacy investment.	✓
Support a structured exchange with business partners.	✓	Enable back-end application integration.	✓
Support partner real-time access to/from applications.	✓	Minimize application complexity.	✓
Support partner real-time access to/from business services.		Minimize enterprise complexity	
Support shared public process flows with partners.		Avoid partner-mandated infrastructures.	
Integrate the internal workflow manager with partner-shared business process flows.		Reduce partner dependency on specific applications.	
		Reduce partner dependency on specific business protocols.	

The primary business driver for choosing this Application pattern is to enable business partner systems to gain direct and real-time access to specific applications. The underlying motivation behind these requirements is to improve the efficiency of interactions between organizations beyond what can be achieved with simple electronic document exchange.

Solution

Figure 10.4 shows this application divided into at least two logical tiers:

- The partner tier represents a set of partner applications that are interested in invoking specific business logic on the exposed application tier.

- The exposed application tier may represent a new application, a modified existing application, or an unmodified existing application. This tier is responsible for implementing the necessary business logic and access to business data. Since this tier is directly exposed across organizational boundaries, it must implement or exploit the necessary security features, such as authentication, authorization, confidentiality, integrity, and logging for non-repudiation purposes. (Refer to the previous Application pattern for an explanation of the arrow for private and public processes.)

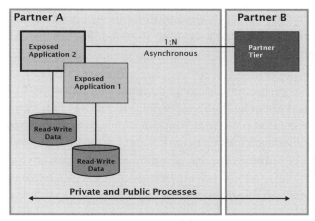

Figure 10.4: This represents the Exposed Application application pattern.

Typically, an asynchronous communication mechanism is used for inter-enterprise integration. The primary reason for this choice, as opposed to using a synchronous communication mechanism, is to minimize the dependency of the service levels of one organization's applications on another organization's applications.

Even though companies agree on certain service levels such as availability and response time, it is hard to ensure, across organizational boundaries, that these service levels are met all the time. The use of an asynchronous communication mechanism ensures that during such a failure, requests can still be sent to partner systems to be processed later. Meanwhile, the application under consideration can continue its processing without having to wait for the response from the partner systems. It also provides a degree of isolation between the two businesses, so that the requesting application can never synchronously demand excessive resources or locks on the partner systems.

Note that asynchronous communication does not necessarily mean delayed response. If the business requirement warrants a quick response, consider fast asynchronous communication, where the response is typically received immediately if the partner system is able to process the request at the time of receipt. If not, the request is processed later. Fast asynchronous communication is becoming increasingly popular for inter-enterprise integration, since it provides most of the benefits of both asynchronous and synchronous communication.

In implementing its capabilities, this Application pattern uses Application Integration techniques and services. In particular, this pattern is based on the Application Integration::Direct Connection application pattern described in Chapter 12.

An asynchronous Message Oriented Middleware (MOM)[4] such as MQSeries (also known as WebSphere MQ) from IBM is typically used for implementing this Application pattern. It is also possible to use synchronous middleware based on standards such as CORBA[5] and DCOM[6]. Most of the time, the dominant player enforces the use of a particular middleware on the rest of the players. Typically, virtual private networks (VPN)[7] are used for interconnection between partner applications, and to implement many of the security features at the network level.

Guidelines for use

Direct integration between applications is typically inflexible, in that any changes to one application might have knock-on effects on other applications. This is especially dangerous when integrating across organizational boundaries. Any changes to the exposed application tier might require changes to many partner systems. Such changes can be both expensive and time-consuming.

Such knock-on effects can be minimized using *message-based adapters* that wrapper the applications in the exposed application tier. Message-based adapters are small programs that convert the mutually agreed-upon messages into API[8] calls to existing or new back-end applications. This layering technique isolates the back-end applications from partner systems and increases flexibility. Any changes to these back-end applications would only affect the adapter, as long as there is no need to change the mutually agreed-upon messages.

The message definition should be generalized to further promote flexibility. In other words, messages should not be tightly coupled with back-end application APIs. Rather, the message should capture all the necessary information required for the logical interaction across business boundaries. Such generalizations will help organizations cope with changes to the back-end application API without having to change the agreed-upon message format.

Benefits

The common Message Oriented Middleware (MOM) enforced by dominant partners is a key enabler of this Application pattern today. The key features delivered by MOM are guaranteed delivery and "once and once only" delivery of messages. In future, open standards such as HTTP might play a more significant role in the guaranteed delivery of messages between organizations.

Limitations

As mentioned earlier, this Application pattern typically requires the use of common middleware among all the participating partners. As a result, you lose flexibility in connecting to business partners that might have different IT infrastructure capabilities. Hence, this Application pattern can be inflexible.

This pattern implements a point-to-point interface between the partner systems and the exposed application tier. Hence, it cannot be used for the intelligent routing of requests, for the decomposition and re-composition of requests, or for invoking a complex business-process workflow as a result of a request from a partner system. Under such circumstances, consider the more advanced Application patterns discussed later in this chapter.

Putting the pattern to use

An auto insurance portal enables customers to compare quotes from many insurance companies at a single Web site. Customers are asked to enter automobile details, driving history, and the terms and conditions of the insurance coverage requested. The portal ships this information to many insurance companies, soliciting their best quotes. The insurance portal promises to gather more than 10 quotes in an hour's time. All participating insurance companies are asked to integrate with the portal using a common MOM.

A small regional insurance company wants to participate in this new sales channel. It currently has an online quote engine that can be directly integrated with the portal using an adapter. The Exposed Application pattern is an ideal solution for this simple integration problem, since only two applications are involved, and the interactions with the portal at this time are limited to providing online quotes.

The Exposed Business Services application pattern

The Exposed Business Services application pattern structures a system design that exposes specific services that can be directly invoked by partner systems across organizational boundaries.

Business and IT drivers

Table 10.5 summarizes the business and IT drivers for this pattern.

Table 10.5: *Business and IT drivers for the Exposed Business Services application pattern*

Business drivers		IT drivers	
Improve the organizational efficiency.	✓	Leverage existing skills.	✓
Reduce the latency of business events.	✓	Leverage the legacy investment.	✓
Support a structured exchange with business partners.	✓	Enable back-end application integration.	✓
Support partner real-time access to/from applications.	✓	Minimize application complexity.	✓
Support partner real-time access to/from business services.	✓	Minimize enterprise complexity	✓
Support shared public process flows with partners.		Avoid partner-mandated infrastructures.	
Integrate the internal workflow manager with partner-shared business process flows.		Reduce partner dependency on specific applications.	✓
		Reduce partner dependency on specific business protocols	

The primary business driver for choosing this Application pattern is to enable business partner systems to gain direct access to specific business services. These services, when invoked, may in turn trigger multiple tasks on many back-end applications. In other words, business requirements cannot be met by simple integration with a single back-end application, as is the case with the Exposed Application pattern.

Consider the previous example of integration between an auto insurance portal and a small regional insurance company. Assume that the insurance company wants to participate in online sales of auto insurance. An online sales request submitted by the portal will trigger several business tasks, such as the verification of driving history, a credit check, an appointment with the nearest office to verify the condition of the automobile, policy processing, and billing. Under this scenario, there is a need to trigger multiple tasks on many back-end applications as a result of a single online sales request.

A point-to-point interface between partner systems and many back-end applications increases complexity and maintenance cost. The Exposed Business Services application pattern can be used to reduce the total cost of ownership by implementing a hub-and-spoke architecture instead of a point-to-point architecture between partner systems and back-end applications.

Solution

In this application pattern, shown in Figure 10.5, there are at least three logical tiers:

- The partner tier represents a set of partner applications that are interested in invoking specific services on the exposed business services tier.

- The exposed business services tier receives requests from multiple partner systems and intelligently routes them to the appropriate back-end applications. It is also responsible for breaking down compound requests into several simpler requests and routing them to multiple back-end systems. Finally, it is responsible for message transformation and managing different levels of security. In doing so, it typically uses a local read-only database to store routing, decomposition, re-composition, and transformation rules. These functions allow for one level of implementation of the private process rules employed in the later Application patterns. This tier typically implements minimal business logic; the majority of the logic is concentrated in the back-end application tier.

- The back-end application tiers (as well as the private and public processes) are the same as those in the previous patterns.

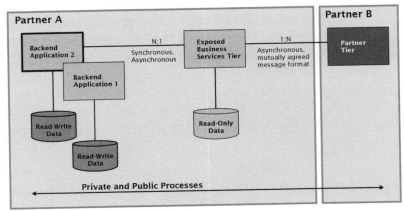

Figure 10.5: This represents the Exposed Business Services application pattern.

This Application pattern is usually implemented using an asynchronous MOM pre-scribed by dominant players over a VPN. This Application pattern leverages many of the common services observed in the Process-Focused Application Integration patterns described in Chapter 12. One of the critical nodes that make up the ex-posed business services tier is a message broker node that can perform intelligent routing, message transformation, decomposition, and re-composition. The charac-teristics of this broker node are further elaborated in the Application Integra-tion::Broker application pattern in Chapter 12. Message brokers are typically implemented using rules-based products such as MQSeries Integrator (also known as WebSphere MQ Integrator)[9].

Guidelines for use

Mutually agreed-upon messages should truly represent the electronic service being offered and should not be tied closely to the back-end applications being invoked. This requires an even broader perspective in defining mutually agreed-upon mes-sages compared to the Exposed Application pattern. Such generalization would fur-ther promote flexibility in changing or replacing back-end applications without significantly affecting partner systems.

Benefits

This Application pattern can leverage investments already made in enterprise appli-cation integration to extend them beyond organizational boundaries. The use of the exposed business services tier isolates the internal business processes and back-end implementation details from the partner systems, and vice versa. This loosely coupled architecture makes it easy to change, replace, or add back-end applications without heavily affecting partner systems. This increases maintainability and reduces the total cost of ownership.

Limitations

This Application pattern currently implies the use of common Message Oriented Middleware among all the participating partners. As a result, you lose flexibility in connecting to business partners that might have different IT infrastructure capabilities. Hence this Application pattern can be somewhat rigid.

Corporations typically have special agreements with different business partners. We call such special agreements *business protocols*. When enterprise integration approaches are extended outside the company, as with this Application pattern, you must be able to handle different business protocols with different business partners. This might require additional hand-crafted protocol-management code for each partner. Under such circumstances, consider a more advanced Application pattern, such as the Managed Public Processes application pattern discussed next.

Putting the pattern to use

A small manufacturer is contracted to produce a set of engine parts for a major industrial company that manufactures aircraft engines. The contract specifies not only the product to be produced, but also the mechanisms for scheduling production, reporting the production status, and producing the shipment status. In addition, the small manufacturer is required to participate in the production planning process. The aircraft engine company has an internal message-queuing network and specifies as part of the agreement that partners must communicate with it over the same MOM.

The small engine-parts manufacturer has a production scheduling application that provides production status, and another application that generates shipping reports. The requirement to participate in production planning requires data to be extracted on demand from these back-end applications. To meet these requirements, the small manufacturer chooses the Exposed Business Services application pattern.

～ The Managed Public Processes application pattern

The Managed Public Processes application pattern structures a system design that handles the management of shared business processes between business partners.

Business and IT drivers

Table 10.6 summarizes the business and IT drivers for this pattern.

Table 10.6: *Business and IT drivers for the Managed Public Processes application pattern*

Business drivers		IT drivers	
Improve the organizational efficiency.	✓	Leverage existing skills.	✓
Reduce the latency of business events.	✓	Leverage the legacy investment.	✓
Support a structured exchange with business partners.	✓	Enable back-end application integration.	✓
Support partner real-time access to/from applications.	✓	Minimize application complexity.	✓
Support partner real-time access to/from business services.	✓	Minimize enterprise complexity	✓
Support shared public process flows with partners.	✓	Avoid partner-mandated infrastructures.	✓
Integrate the internal workflow manager with partner-shared business process flows.		Reduce partner dependency on specific applications.	✓
		Reduce partner dependency on specific business protocols.	✓

It is typical for corporations to enter into special agreements with different business partners. In business-to-business electronic commerce, there is a need to agree not only on the traditional terms and conditions, but also on IT issues such as the following:

- Roles assumed by different parties

- Valid sequences of requests

- Electronic message formats

- Communication protocols to be used

- Security issues such as authentication, encryption, and non-repudiation

- Service level agreements such as response time and availability

- Error-handling procedures

The specific details of these business protocols vary from one set of partners to another. They can also vary over a period of time between the same set of partners. The primary business driver for choosing this Application pattern is to support different business protocols with different business partners.

All of the Application patterns considered so far require a common set of middleware and IT infrastructure among the participants. For example, the Document Exchange application pattern enforces the use of a particular VAN among all of the partners. Similarly, dominant partners enforce the use of a common Message Oriented Middleware in most of the implementations of the Exposed Application and Exposed Business Services application patterns. Such requirements have been blamed by some for the slow acceptance of inter-business integration prior to the emergence of the Internet. Along with the Internet, several standards-based communication protocols, such as HTTP and SMTP,[10] have emerged. By using such standards-based protocols, companies can achieve complete independence from their business partners in implementing their back-end applications and choosing their IT infrastructure.

All of the business and IT drivers listed for the Exposed Business Services application pattern apply here, as well.

Solution

This application pattern is divided into at least three logical tiers:

- The public process rules tier receives requests from multiple business partners. It is responsible for ensuring that the agreed-upon business protocols with all these partners are satisfied. It maps the external communication protocols into internal communication protocols before forwarding the request to the back-end application tier. For example, an agreement with a particular business partner might require receiving requests using secure HTTPS[11] protocol. Such a request might need to be converted into a MQSeries message before being passed to the back-end application tier.

In addition, this tier is responsible for implementing the necessary security features, such as authentication, authorization, encryption, message integrity, and non-repudiation. These security checks are much more important in this Application pattern than in the ones mentioned so far in this chapter, since this pattern allows for receiving requests over the Internet. Finally, this tier is also responsible for sending the required response back, in which it typically relies on the response received from the back-end application tier. A single public process rules tier can be used to support multiple partners, each employing different business protocols.

If integration with internal business applications is complex, this tier might include a message broker node to handle rules for private processes such as message decomposition, routing, and transformation. The characteristics of this broker node are further elaborated by the Application Integration::Broker application pattern in Chapter 12.

- The partner and back-end application tiers are the same as those for the previous pattern.

The public process rules tier is best implemented by using middleware products that can generate business protocol management code by interpreting electronically defined contracts. IBM's WebSphere Partner Agreement Manager[12] implements such a framework.

The Managed Public Processes application pattern is shown in Figure 10.6.

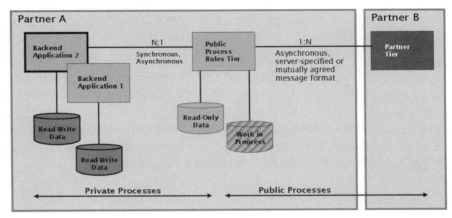

Figure 10.6: The Managed Public Processes application pattern is divided into at least three logical tiers.

Guidelines for use

Simple implementations involving a few business protocols with a limited number of business partners can be implemented using hand-crafted protocol-management code. Typically, such applications are written to run on a standard Web application server. The emerging protocol to consider in this arena is SOAP. [13]

For more extensive implementations, consider capturing the details of business protocols such as roles, valid sequence of messages, message format, and security issues using an electronic contract. These electronic contracts are called *Trading Partner Agreements (TPAs)*. They can be expressed using an XML-based language [14] such as tpaML.

A TPA describes all the valid, visible, and enforceable interactions between the parties. It is independent of the internal business processes and back-end applications of each party. Each partner builds its own internal business process to satisfy these external TPAs and interfaces them to the rest of its business processes and back-end applications. The intent is to provide a high-level specification that can be easily understood by humans, and yet is precise enough for enforcement by computers.

TPAs can be compiled into business protocol management code that implements interaction rules in each party's system. The information in the TPA is not a complete description of the application, but only a description of the interactions between the parties. The application must be designed and programmed in the usual manner. Use of TPAs increases flexibility, speeds the time to market, and avoids error-prone hand-coding, since changes can be made to the TPA, and then protocol management code can be generated from it. Further details on TPAs and tpaML can be found at http://www.xml.org/xmlorg_resources/b2bxml.shtml.

To increase the ease of interoperability between multiple business partners, standardized business-to-business protocols such as Open Buying on the Internet (OBI) [15] and RossettaNet [16] should be used.

Benefits

The public process rules tier completely isolates the internal systems and business processes from external parties. Hence, it ensures that each party maintains complete independence from the other, both in the IT infrastructure and in the nature of the business processes resulting. This results in a highly flexible architecture.

Limitations

This Application pattern can exploit universally accepted communication protocols such as HTTP and SMTP for integration between partners. However, unlike MOM technologies such as MQSeries, these protocols do not guarantee reliable "once and once only" message delivery. Hence, the use of MOM techniques can still be found in industries and business scenarios where reliability is of the utmost importance. Note, however, that improvements in the reliability provided by these open technologies can be expected over the next few years.

Even though this Application pattern can handle special agreements with different business partners and can ensure that each party maintains complete independence in terms of IT infrastructure, back-end applications, and business process, it cannot map long-running external transactions to internal business processes and workflow. Under such circumstances, consider more advanced Application patterns such as the Managed Public and Private Processes application pattern, discussed next.

Putting the pattern to use

A producer of computer parts wants to integrate with the supply chains of several PC manufacturers. Because the IT industry has jointly developed a supply chain standard called RosettaNet, and PC manufacturers support this standard, the producer of computer parts decides to use RosettaNet to integrate with these supply chains.

RosettaNet is a sophisticated B2B protocol requiring considerable effort to implement. A public process rules tier is needed to map it into interactions with the internal applications and processes of the computer parts producer. Hence, the company chooses the Managed Public Processes application pattern for this deployment. Although the business-to-business processes are sophisticated, the integration with internal applications is manageable using messaging to the back-end application tier.

~ The Managed Public and Private Processes application pattern

The Managed Public and Private Processes application pattern structures a system design that handles different business protocols with different business partners and maps long-running external transactions to internal business processes and workflow.

Business and IT drivers

All the business and IT drivers listed under the Managed Public Processes application pattern apply here as well. Furthermore, long-running transactions need to be accommodated across organizational boundaries. Dan and Parr observed that transactions spanning multiple independent organizations have different characteristics compared to traditional ACID transactions executed inside a single organizational boundary.[17] They are typically composed of many related interactions dispersed in time, resulting in long-running conversations. Such long-running conversations are particularly important since very little can be assumed about the target execution environment, response time, network availability, and the need for human intervention to complete the request. This results in the need to map such long-running external transactions to internal business processes and workflows.

Table 10.7 summarizes the business and IT drivers for this pattern.

Table 10.7: *Business and IT drivers for*		
the Managed Public and Private Processes application pattern		
Business drivers		**IT drivers**	
Improve the organizational efficiency.	✓	Leverage existing skills.	✓
Reduce the latency of business events.	✓	Leverage the legacy investment.	✓
Support a structured exchange with business partners.	✓	Enable back-end application integration.	✓
Support partner real-time access to/from applications.	✓	Minimize application complexity.	✓
Support partner real-time access to/from business services.	✓	Minimize enterprise complexity	✓
Support shared public process flows with partners.	✓	Avoid partner-mandated infrastructures.	✓
Integrate the internal workflow manager with partner-shared business process flows.	✓	Reduce partner dependency on specific applications.	✓
		Reduce partner dependency on specific business protocols.	✓

For example, agreed-upon inter-business workflows (public process rules) can be defined to govern the long-running transactions comprising entire business process cycles (such as submit RFQ—receive price quotation—issue purchase order—manage fulfillment). Private process rules can then capture lower-level workflows, including all human and machine interactions needed to complete each major step in the business process ("approve purchase order," for example). This "local" workflow will typically employ application integration techniques, including message brokering and application adapters, to execute its function.

Solution

This Application pattern, shown in Figure 10.7, has at least four logical tiers:

- The public process rules tier receives requests from multiple business partners. It is responsible for ensuring that all the agreed-upon business protocols are satisfied. In doing so, it implements all the features described under the Managed Public Processes application pattern with one exception:

Instead of passing external requests to the back-end application tier directly, it passes them to the private process rules tier.

- The private process rules tier is responsible for mapping external long-running transactions to internal business processes and workflows. To manage workflows efficiently, it combines the activities of a process, all the people in the organization, and the infrastructure (such as computers and programs). In other words, it maintains the status of the long-running transaction and moves work from one resource to another based on the internal business process. (Resources in this context refer to people in the organization and the business applications.)

- The partner and back-end application tiers are the same as those for the previous pattern.

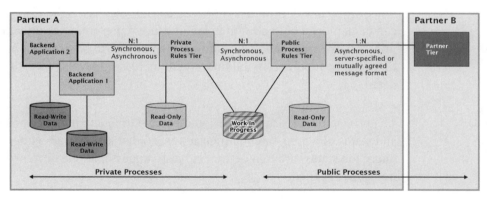

Figure 10.7: The Managed Public and Private Processes application pattern has at least four logical tiers.

The private process rules tier leverages most of the process-focused application integration services observed in Chapter 12. It is often a manifestation of the Application Integration::Managed Process application pattern, also elaborated in Chapter 12. You can combine MQSeries Integrator, MQSeries Workflow (also known as WebSphere Process Manager) and/or the "business flow manager" component of the WebSphere Business Integrator to implement this tier.

Guidelines for use

The success of the Managed Public and Private Processes application pattern relies heavily on the ability to define generic inter-enterprise business processes and workflows. These workflows vary between different sets of business partners. Over time, these business processes change between the same set of business partners. To accommodate this dynamic environment, the flow dependency should be separated from the application. Such a separation allows for changing the workflow without affecting the applications. A message-based workflow management system should be used to define and implement these inter-enterprise workflows.

A holistic approach must be taken in defining inter-enterprise business processes and how they map to the internal workflow. It begins with a description of the roles and responsibilities, task flows and processes, and data definitions and documents underlying the joint business processes. The approach then employs a set of tools to transform these descriptions into a consistent and coherent set of message definitions, workflow definitions, directory entries, database schemas, and so on, which can be deployed onto a runtime architecture representing a software implementation of these processes. This "ultimate" approach to business-to-business interactions can be modified in the future with increasing levels of depth and technical detail.

The private process rules tier should be able to maintain the correlation ID, history, and status of a long-running transaction, so that an external party can effectively query the status of a transaction and also request that one or more of these interactions be cancelled.

Refer to the previous Application pattern for guidelines on expressing business protocols electronically using TPAs.

Benefits

This Application pattern provides all the benefits of the Managed Public Processes application pattern, while further enhancing the complete independence gained with respect to the business processes. Internal business processes and workflows can be changed without affecting external business partners.

The principle of message-based workflow management separates the workflow information from applications. This results in a highly flexible architecture where business process flow can be changed without affecting applications. In addition, this enables the reuse of applications as software components in other processes. Furthermore, it allows applications to be replaced or changed without affecting the overall workflow. The combination of flexibility and reuse results in significant cost savings.

Limitations

Implementing a truly generic and complete business-to-business integration capability is a significant and complex undertaking that requires a considerable amount of effort, time, and resources. Also, many legacy applications have built-in workflow. Separating flow information from such back-end systems is complex, time-consuming, and in some cases, might not even be possible.

Putting the pattern to use

Consider the example from the previous Application pattern, where a producer of computer parts wants to integrate with the supply chains of several PC manufacturers. The computer parts producer might have a large number of business processes controlling production, parts inventory management, procurement, and other critical activities that need to be integrated with the supply chain. It recognizes that this B2B integration requires more than simple application mapping. Long-running inter-business workflow must be managed and mapped into private processes. To meet these requirements, it chooses the Managed Public and Private Processes application pattern.

Step 6d: Identify Application patterns in the FECS solution

Step 3 of the case study, discussed in Chapter 4, identifies the existence of an Extended Enterprise business pattern within the FECS solution. A more detailed look at the customer financing functions brings out a few key requirements:

- The interactions between the FECS solution and the financial institution are codified using a Trading Partner Agreement (TPA).

- The external financial institution publishes standard application programming interfaces to its financing application.

- These APIs can be accessed by using the Simple Object Access Protocol (SOAP) across a secure HTTP connection.

From a business perspective, the chosen architecture should be able to support shared business process flows with multiple financial institutions. This can be achieved by introducing a public process rules tier that isolates the internal FECS business processes from external business processes. From an IT perspective, the connectivity between FECS and the financial institution should not mandate the use of certain middleware on either party. This independence can be achieved by using standard-based universal protocols such as HTTP and SOAP.

Matching these requirements to the business and IT drivers of the various Application patterns for Extended Enterprise reveals that the Extended Enterprise::Managed Public Process application pattern would be required to automate this Business pattern. This is shown in Figure 10.8.

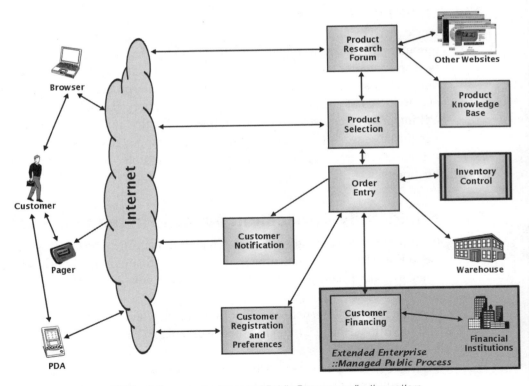

Figure 10.8: The FECS solution uses the Managed Public Process application pattern.

References

[1] Electronic Data Interchange (EDI)—A standard format for exchanging business data. An EDI message contains a string of data elements, each of which represents a singular fact, such as a price, product model number, and so forth, separated by a delimiter. The entire string is called a *data segment*. One or more data segments framed by a header and trailer form an EDI transaction set.

[2] Value Added Network (VAN)—A networking service that leases communication lines to subscribers and provides extra capability such as security, error detection, guaranteed message delivery, and a message buffer.

[3] EDI translation packages—Convert EDI messages from (and to) flat files, into a usable format for an enterprise's applications.

[4] Message Oriented Middleware (MOM)—Provides program-to-program communications by message passing. It provides an infrastructure that supports reliable and scalable high-performance distributed application networks.

[5] Common Object Request Broker Architecture (CORBA)—An architecture and specification for creating, distributing, and managing distributed program objects in a network. It allows programs at different locations and developed by different vendors to communicate in a network through an "interface broker." CORBA was developed by a consortium of vendors through the Object Management Group (OMG). It currently includes over 500 member companies.

[6] Distributed Component Object Model (DCOM)—A set of Microsoft concepts and program interfaces in which a client program object can request services from server program objects on other computers in a network.

[7] virtual private network (VPN)—A private data network that makes use of the public telecommunication infrastructure. The idea of the VPN is to give companies the same capabilities as a leased private network at a much lower cost by using the shared public infrastructure. This is

achieved by encrypting data before sending it through the public network, and decrypting it at the receiving end.

[8] Application Programming Interface (API)—Defines how programmers use a particular feature provided by an application.

[9] MQSeries Integrator—Combines a one-to-many connectivity model, plus transformation, intelligent routing, and information flow modeling. It facilitates the development of new application services that integrate the functions of multiple, disparate existing business systems. More information can be found at http://www.ibm.com/software/ts/mqseries/integrator/

[10] Simple Mail Transfer Protocol (SMTP)—Used for sending and receiving e-mails between servers.

[11] HTTPS—*See* Secure Hypertext Transfer Protocol in the Glossary

[12] WebSphere Partner Agreement Manager—Enables multiple partners to participate in shared business processes that can be partially or fully integrated depending on business needs. More information can be found at http://www.ibm.com/software/webservers/pam/

[13] Simple Object Access Protocol (SOAP)—Provides a way for a program running on one kind of operating system to communicate with a program on the same or another kind of operating system by using HTTP protocol and Extensible Markup Language (XML) as the mechanisms for information exchange.

[14] XML—*See* Extensible Markup Language in the Glossary

[15] Open Buying on the Internet (OBI)—A proposed standard for business-to-business purchasing on the Internet, aimed particularly at high-volume, low-cost-per-item transactions. More information can be found at http://www.openbuy.org

[16] RossettaNet—An organization set up by leading IT companies to define and implement a common set of standards for e-business. RosettaNet is

defining a common parts dictionary so that different companies can define the same product the same way. It is also defining up to 100 e-business transaction processes and standardizing them. Because RosettaNet is supported by all or most of the major companies in the IT industry, its standards are expected to be widely adopted. More information can be found at http://www.rosettanet.org

[17] Dan, A., and F. Parr. "An object implementation of network-centric business service applications (NCBAs)." September 1997. Atlanta, GA: OOPSLA Business Object Workshop.

11

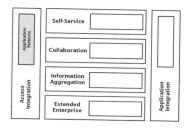

Application patterns for Access Integration

The Access Integration pattern captures the essence of providing users consistent and seamless access to various applications using different mechanisms. It becomes relevant when:

- Users need access to multiple applications and information sources, without every application requiring its own sign-on to establish a separate security context.

- These applications need to be accessed using multiple devices, such as fat clients, browsers, voice response units, mobile devices, and PDAs.

- These applications need to have a common look and feel.

- The user wishes to customize the choice of applications and how they are presented.

The Access Integration pattern

Some of these requirements can be observed within an Application pattern such as Self-Service::Router or Self-Service::Decomposition. These Application patterns provide a way for users to access various back-end applications using a single presentation mechanism. Similarly, Access Integration patterns can be used to enable a more complex e-business solution composed of multiple Business patterns. For example, a browser-based, personalized portal can be developed by combining applications that automate the Self-Service business pattern and the Collaboration business pattern. This personalized portal might then need to be made accessible via mobile devices.

A study of several e-business solutions that have successfully met these challenging requirements reveals the use of some recurring, common services. The objective is to externalize these services and make them selectable by the developers of the integrated solution. This chapter describes these common services and two selected Application patterns for Access Integration that are composed of one or more of these services.

Common services for the Access Integration pattern

The Application patterns that automate the Access Integration pattern are different from the Application patterns that automate Business patterns, in that they are made up of a number of common services. These services, in themselves, do not provide end-to-end business value if they are deployed in isolation of the Application patterns used to automate Business patterns. Instead, they can be useful for composing complex solutions by front-ending a single or multiple Application patterns. These services are designed to work together to implement an Access Integration pattern, whereas the Application patterns for a given Business pattern are typically mutually exclusive when they are used to solve a business problem.

The Access Integration patterns observed in practice are composed of the following services:

- Device Support

- Presentation

- Personalization

- Security and Administration

The Device Support service

The Device Support service enables users of a wide range of devices (such as clients that support graphical user interfaces, clients that support Internet browsers, and pervasive devices) to access the same set of applications. From a business perspective, this service increases the reach of business applications. From an IT standpoint, this service avoids having to modify the application for additional types of devices. This allows for a single code base, which enhances the organization's ability to maintain the application and make changes to it. It also helps to reduce the total cost of ownership of the application.

The best practice for implementing the Device Support service is to externalize it from individual applications. This is accomplished by implementing a Device Support node that accepts data from existing applications in some common format (such as XML) and transforms it into a format that is compatible with the user's device type through a process called *transcoding*.[1] The data is then sent to the user device using a device- and/or a network-specific protocol. For example, when the client is a WAP[2]-enabled phone, the program that accesses the back-end system typically assembles the data as an XML document. This document is then transcoded into a Wireless Markup Language (WML) [3] document that is sent to the phone using the Wireless Application Protocol (WAP) for transmission across a GSM network.

Consider a travel reservation Web site providing air, hotel, car rental, and vacation reservation services, which can currently be accessed via a browser. The owners of this Web site would like to extend their reach by enabling the same services to be accessed via WAP-enabled mobile phones that can render WML. Instead of developing a Web site tailored for mobile phones, this company can use transcoding techniques on the current Web site to make it accessible from mobile phones.

The Presentation service

The Presentation service is the foundation of a universal desktop for all the Web-based applications in an enterprise. It provides a common look and feel, as well as language transparency, across multiple applications.

As personal, departmental, enterprise, and inter-enterprise applications continue to expand, there is a need to provide a managed "window on the world" to reduce user-perceived complexity and the resultant education and training costs. In addition, increasing globalization requires that the same information or service be delivered in a variety of languages.

The best practice for achieving these goals is to clearly separate the content from the presentation style at the content-creation stage. Technologies such as Cascading

Style Sheets (CSS) [4] can be used to establish organization-wide presentation styles, which can be applied to all the static and dynamic content served by that organization's Web applications. With this approach, when a presentation style needs to be changed, it is not necessary to change all the Web pages; instead, only the appropriate CSS needs to be updated. This can also reduce the total cost of ownership of Web applications.

A more sophisticated separation of content and presentation styles might use technologies such as XML/XSL.[5] Here, content is described using XML documents, and the presentation style is expressed using one or more XSL-based style sheets. This separation enables the same content to be presented differently to different users by merely applying a different style sheet, without any changes to the content.

Consider an online brokerage firm that serves investors of varying experience and interests. Professional stockbrokers who use this site expect to see a detailed company analysis on a single page so that they can make quick and informed investment decisions. Small investors, on the other hand, might prefer the company analysis to be presented in a more approachable format that provides a high-level analysis, but does not bombard them with too much technical data. Both these versions of the company analysis page can be assembled by applying different style sheets to the same underlying content. This technique eliminates the need for creating and maintaining different versions of the same content, and thus again reduces the total cost of ownership. It also ensures the consistency of the information being disseminated across presentation styles.

The globalization of the economy and the universal reach of e-business applications demand multiple language support. This is not only required to support worldwide customers, but also to ensure equal access to corporate information for all employees. Machine translation technologies such as WebSphere Translation Server [6] can be used to translate text from one language to another in real-time at a fraction of the cost of professional translators.

The Presentation service is used by the Device Support service and the Personalization service. For example, the Device Support service can leverage the Presentation service to ensure that the appropriate images are downloaded to the mobile phone, based on the physical dimensions of that device. It is clear that these presentation capabilities can be leveraged by many applications in an organization. If each application takes a custom approach toward achieving its goals, the IT costs for maintaining, supporting, and enhancing these applications will eventually become prohibitive.

The Personalization service

The Personalization service provides a number of approaches that allow users or enterprises to shape the choice, style, and format of their selected applications. Personalization may be done at many levels, including individual, group, and role. This service relies on other services, especially Presentation and Security.

There are significant productivity benefits to be gained by allowing users to specify their preferred way of navigating to applications, interacting with applications, and being provided with information. In this way users get what they want rather than being overwhelmed by lots of information that they are not interested in. The enterprise, meanwhile, wants to find the most acceptable way to limit (disable) services based on employee, customer, or contractual profiles. There are also significant IT benefits to be gained from allowing business domain experts to dynamically update personalization and business rules to respond to changing business requirements.

The Personalization service performs several key functions, including the following:

1. Identify the user.

2. Retrieve the user's profile. A profile is a stored set of information that describes a user's interests, role in an organization, entitlements, or some other set of descriptors that are important to the Web site owner. This profile may also be enhanced by:

   - Explicit profiling, in which users are asked to indicate their interests by completing a short questionnaire or performing some other explicit action.

   - Implicit profiling, in which the system monitors the actions of a user (pages viewed, items purchased, and so on) and infers the interests of the user, instead of asking him or her for information.

3. Select the content that matches the user's preferences. There are several approaches to making the content decision:

- Simple filtering, in which the site displays content based on predefined groups of users.

- Rules engines, in which the site owner defines a set of business rules that determine what category of content is shown to a user of a certain profile.

- Inference engines, in which sophisticated statistical approaches and other forms of intelligent software are used to extract trends from the behavior of users.

- Collaborative filtering, in which the user rates a selection of products. These ratings are then compared with the ratings of other users so that recommendations can be made based on similarities and differences.

4. Retrieve the content and assemble the page for display to the user.

To achieve these goals across multiple applications, the high-level personalization logic must be externalized from individual applications. Such externalization enables easier integration with other applications in the future.

The Security and Administration service

The Security and Administration service helps to structure a system design that allows users to access multiple applications and information sources with a single security model and through a single security interaction.

We are all familiar with having to remember different user IDs and passwords to access different applications. These different authentication requirements inconvenience users by requiring them to remember multiple ID-and-password combinations, and by forcing them to sign on multiple times to access different systems. In addition, some systems might use authentication techniques that are not based on user ID and password.

The primary business driver for this service is to eliminate these user inconveniences while continuing to protect the security of enterprise data and applications. A key requirement is for a single sign-on, so that a user logs on once to gain access to all the applications and data sources. Another key requirement is access management that enables the installation to limit access based on a user profile and an organization's policies. Because many different applications are made accessible to many different users or groups, access management is typically role-based and hierarchical. For example, a person who assumes a new managerial role must have instant access to a set of applications derived from his or her updated profile information.

The best practice for achieving these requirements is to externalize both authentication [7] and authorization services [8] from individual applications into a single, common Security and Administration node. This is often achieved by developing an enterprise-wide directory of users and their access permissions, using technologies such as LDAP [9] directories. The success of this service relies on the ability of individual applications to take advantage of an external authentication and authorization mechanism.

The externalization of authentication and authorization mechanisms eliminates the need to duplicate such functionality inside every application. In addition, it can facilitate enterprise-wide user administration, instead of having these activities performed at an individual application level.

The ability to take advantage of this service across multiple applications relies largely on an enterprise-wide agreement on authentication and authorization requirements. This agreement is not limited to the technology and the protocols to be used; it also includes issues such as determining the information that is sufficient to authenticate a user, specifying formats for the user ID and password, and setting the password expiration date.

When different applications have separate user profiles, the developers of these applications have the luxury of defining the authentication requirements based on their needs and the sensitivity of the data their applications deal with. However, when authentication services are externalized to enable a single sign-on, the services provided by this externalized tier must be satisfactory to all the applications that rely on it. Hence, enterprise-wide security standards must be established.

Selected Access Integration application patterns

Application patterns for Access Integration are composed of the services just discussed. Based on the specific installation needs, you can mix and match these services to facilitate consistent and seamless access to multiple applications. The rest of this chapter presents two commonly observed Application patterns for Access Integration, shown in Figure 11.1.

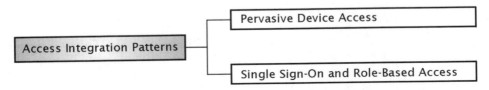

Figure 11.1: These two Access Integration application patterns are the focus of this chapter.

The Pervasive Device Access application pattern

The Pervasive Device Access application pattern provides a structure for extending the reach of individual applications from browsers and fat clients to pervasive devices such as PDAs and mobile phones.

Business and IT drivers

Table 11.1 summarizes the business and IT drivers for this pattern.

Table 11.1: *Business and IT drivers for the Pervasive Device Access application pattern*

Business drivers		IT drivers	
Provide universal access to information and services.	✓	Decrease the time to market.	✓
Provide a single sign on across multiple applications.		Reduce the total cost of ownership.	✓
Provide role-based access to various applications and data.		Reduce the user administration cost.	

Striving to provide universal access to information and applications is often the primary business driver for choosing this Application pattern. The primary IT driver is to quickly extend the reach of applications to new device types without having to modify every individual application.

Solution

This Application pattern, shown in Figure 11.2, uses the Device Support service and the Security and Administration service. It has three logical tiers:

- The pervasive device tier represents devices such as PDAs and mobile phones that can render data formats such as WML and iMode.[10]

- The pervasive device access tier receives requests from pervasive devices and converts them into the appropriate requests that can be understood by existing applications. It then converts the responses from these applications into formats that can be rendered by the pervasive device. The rules governing the transcoding from one format to the other are captured by the meta data in Figure 11.2. In providing pervasive device support, this tier implements the Device Support service for protocol adaptation and data stream transcoding, and the Security and Administration service to ensure that users can achieve a single sign-on to existing applications.

- The application tier may represent new applications, modified existing applications, or unmodified existing applications. These are predominantly browser-based applications that must be made available on wireless devices. They may represent applications that automate Self-Service, Collaboration, or Information Aggregation business patterns.

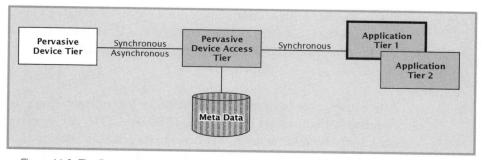

Figure 11.2: The Pervasive Device Access application pattern has three logical tiers.

Consider extending a browser-based application to be accessed by a WAP-enabled mobile phone, which renders WML data over a cellular network. In this scenario, the pervasive device access tier can be implemented using a package such as

WebSphere Everyplace Suite,[11] and divided into a WAP gateway and a transcoding node.

The WAP gateway is responsible for protocol conversion between WAP to HTTP. The gateway must also handle state-management issues, since today's WAP devices don't support cookies.

The transcoding node is responsible for converting the HTML response from the existing browser-based application into a WML response to be sent to the pervasive device. This node usually uses device-specific style sheets to determine what type of information can be made available on the device. For example, an HTML page that displays news items with headlines, summaries, and links to detailed reports obviously does not lend itself to a mobile phone display, so only the headlines and links might be displayed on the phone. Similarly, downloading large icons and images over a wireless network might not be the best use of the low bandwidth available, so you might decide to either completely eliminate graphics or to convert them into optimized image formats such as WBMP (Wireless Bitmap).[12] Device-specific style sheets can capture such content selection, conversion, and elimination criteria.

Guidelines for use

The implementation of this Application pattern calls for a careful examination of the placement of the transcoding logic and its influence on the dialog mapping. Transcoding logic placed within an enterprise's infrastructure (on its Web server) allows flexible or tight control over the mapping of a dialog to the form and size of the access device, such as a mobile phone or a Palm Pilot. This placement assumes a tight linkage of the user community to the enterprise and some IT sophistication to run a wireless infrastructure.

Alternatively, the logic can be placed on the ISP infrastructure, supporting a loose coupling with the target informational Web site. (The device user may access many sites using the same mapping service.) In this case, the owner of the dialogs (the enterprise) provides a device-specific sequence of the dialog, which is then transcoded by the ISP service.

For a detailed discussion on these issues, refer to "Pervasive Computing and the Patterns for e-business" by Leo Marland (ftp://www6.software.ibm.com/software/developer/patterns/pervasive-computing.pdf).

Benefits

This Application pattern allows users to have considerable choice of devices for accessing their applications and data sources.

Limitations

This Application pattern is unlikely to optimize the user interface for any particular device type. If optimization is required, then additional application changes will be necessary.

Putting the pattern to use

An insurance company has a team of claims assessors visiting policyholders to check the validity and value of their insurance claims. The claims assessors need frequent and fast access to the policies, claims details, and so on. They also need to initiate contacts with garages and rental car companies through their extended enterprise applications. On the road, the assessors' preferred access is through wireless-connected palmtop devices. At home or in the office, they use laptop computers for general activities like writing reports. Hence, the insurance company chooses the Pervasive Device Access application pattern to extend the existing claims applications to be accessed via palmtop devices.

The Single Sign-On and Role-Based Access application pattern

The Single Sign-On and Role-Based Access application pattern provides a structure for integrating several applications under a portal that provides single sign-on capability and role-based access to certain information and applications.

Business and IT drivers

Table 11.2 summarizes the business and IT drivers for this pattern.

Table 11.2: *Business and IT drivers for the Single Sign-On and Role-Based Access application pattern*

Business drivers		IT drivers	
Provide universal access to information and services.		Decrease the time to market.	
Provide a single sign on across multiple applications.	✓	Reduce the total cost of ownership.	✓
Provide role-based access to various applications and data.	✓	Reduce the user administration cost.	✓

The primary business driver for choosing this Application pattern is to provide seamless access to multiple applications with a single sign-on, while continuing to protect the security of enterprise information and applications. Another key requirement is access management that limits access based on user profiles and an organization's application policies. Based on an application policy and a user's role, it is possible to personalize the welcome page that shows all the applications the user can access.

Solution

This Application pattern, shown in Figure 11.3, uses the Security and Administration service and the Personalization service. It is divided into three logical tiers:

- The client tier represents the user interface client, such as a browser, mobile phone, or PDA.

- The single sign-on and role-based access tier implements the Security and Administration service, which provides a seamless sign-on and access capability across multiple applications. This is achieved by externalizing the authentication mechanism from individual applications. This tier uses a user-profile data store. In most cases, the user profile is read-only, but it can also be read/write to keep track of such things as the last sign-on and the number of invalid sign-on attempts.

  This tier intercepts all sign-on requests, authenticates the user, and establishes a user's credentials upon successful authentication. Subsequently, if the user tries to access another application that also requires a sign-on, the user's credentials will be automatically passed on. Since the target application recognizes the credentials that have already been established, it will refrain from asking the user to sign on again. As a result, a user will be able to sign on once and access all the applications that are integrated using this Application pattern.

This tier also implements the Personalization service, which uses the user profile to determine the user's role. Based on this information, it decides which applications must be made available to that user. This results in the creation of a role-based personalized portal for the user.

- The application tier may represent new applications, modified existing applications, or unmodified existing applications. These applications may automate Self-Service, Collaboration, or Information Aggregation business patterns.

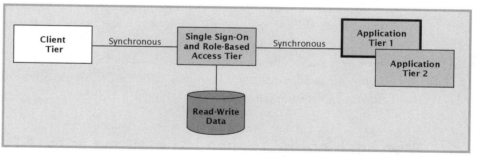

Figure 11.3: The Single Sign-On and Role-Based Access application pattern has three logical tiers.

Guidelines for use

The success of this Application pattern relies on the ability of individual applications to take advantage of an external authentication mechanism. Many legacy systems are not built to use an external authentication mechanism. Instead, they often rely on an internal user profile. Care must be to taken to ensure that all new applications being built or installed are capable of using an external authentication mechanism.

When more than one application relies on this authentication mechanism, it has the potential to be a single point of failure. Hence, care must be taken to ensure that the technology and infrastructure used for this tier is highly available.

Benefits

This pattern reduces the application development cost by avoiding the need for developing authentication services and user profiles in multiple systems. In addition, the user profile can be centrally managed and controlled. For example, when a user's access is revoked in one place, it will be revoked from all the applications. As a result, the system management costs are minimized.

Limitations

Integrating legacy applications that cannot take advantage of external user profiles into this portal could be challenging.

Putting the pattern to use

An insurance company wants to create an Enterprise Information Portal (EIP) that consolidates various applications and information sources and provides a managed window for all customer-facing employees, such as customer service representatives, agents, and brokers. Such a portal must provide single sign-on capability and must personalize the welcome screen based on the user's role. To implement these requirements, the insurance company chooses the Single Sign-On and Role-Based Access application pattern.

Step 6e: Identify Application patterns in the FECS solution

Step 4 of the case study, discussed in Chapter 5, identifies the existence of an Access Integration pattern within the FECS solution. A detailed look at the solution requirements leads to the following architectural decisions:

- There is a need to provide a single sign-on across the multiple applications that automate the different Business patterns. These applications include the product research forum, product selection and order entry, and customer registration and preferences.

- Based on the user role, FECS might need to provide different privileges. For example, only the purchasing director of the end-product manufacturing company can authorize orders exceeding a certain preset limit. Similarly, only purchasing directors can register other users who can place orders on behalf of their respective companies. This requires role-based access to certain functions across multiple applications, such as order entry and customer registration.

- Based on the user preference, the user needs to be notified about the status of the order either via e-mail or pager. Additionally, the user can check the status of the order proactively by logging on to the site using either a PDA or a browser.

These requirements can be implemented using the Access Integration::Single Sign-On and Role-Based Access application pattern to implement the single sign-on and role-based personalization functions, and the Access Integration::Pervasive Device Access application pattern to implement the device support for pervasive devices. This is shown in Figure 11.4.

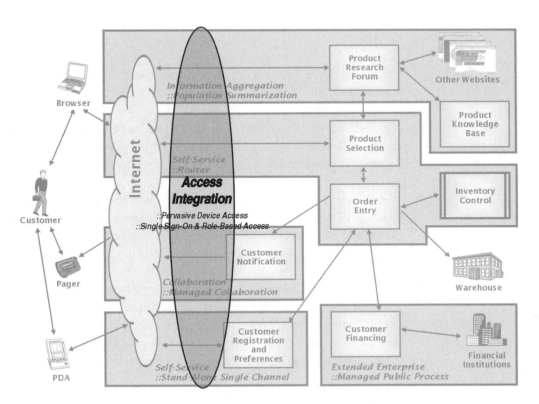

Figure 11.4: Access Integration application patterns are added to the FECS solution.

References

[1]   transcoding—Bridges data across multiple formats, markup languages, and devices. In addition, it adapts, reformats, and filters content to make it suitable for pervasive devices. Products such as WebSphere Transcoding Publisher implement this technology. More information can be found at http://www.ibm.com/software/webservers/transcoding/

[2]   Wireless Application Protocol (WAP)—A specification for a communication protocol to standardize the way that wireless devices, such as cellular telephones and radio transceivers, can be used for Internet access.

[3]   Wireless Markup Language (WML)—A language that allows the text portions of Web pages to be presented on cellular telephone and PDAs via wireless access. WML is part of the Wireless Application Protocol (WAP).

[4]   Cascading Style Sheets (CSS)—A simple mechanism for adding presentation style to Web documents.

[5]   XSL—Extensible Stylesheet Language is a language for creating style sheets. It describes how XML data is to be transformed and formatted before it is presented to a user or passed on to another system.

[6]   WebSphere Translation Server—A machine-translation offering that can help companies remove language as a barrier to global communication and e-commerce. More information can be found at http://www.ibm.com/software/speech/enterprise/ep_8.html

[7]   authentication—The process of determining whether someone or something is, in fact, who or what it is declared to be. In private and public computer networks (including the Internet), authentication is commonly done through the use of sign-on passwords. Knowledge of the password is assumed to guarantee that the user is authentic.

[8]   authorization—The process of giving someone permission to do or have something. A system administrator defines which users are allowed access to the system and what use privileges they are given

(such as access to which file directories, hours of access, and amount of allocated storage space). Logically, authorization is preceded by authentication.

[9] Lightweight Directory Access Protocol (LDAP)—A software protocol for enabling anyone to locate organizations, individuals, and other resources (such as files and devices in a network), whether on the Internet or on a corporate intranet.

[10] iMode—The packet-based service for mobile phones offered by Japan's leader in wireless technology, NTT DoCoMo. Unlike most of the key players in the wireless arena, iMode eschews WAP and uses a simplified version of HTML, and it uses Compact Wireless Markup Language (CWML) instead of WML.

[11] WebSphere Everyplace Suite—A comprehensive, integrated software platform for extending the reach of e-business applications, enterprise data, and Internet content into the realm of pervasive computing. More information can be found at http://www.ibm.com/pvc/products/wes/

[12] Wireless Bitmap (WBMP)—A graphic format optimized for mobile computing devices. It is part of the WAP specification.

C H A P T E R **12**

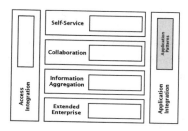

Application patterns for Application Integration

In taking stock of corporate data processing, it becomes clear that:

- The majority of the core business processes have been automated. For example, inventory systems, online banking, claim settlement, and ERP systems form the basis of corporations' daily operations.

- The codification of corporate operational information is almost complete. Data quality and consistency issues persist, but the repetitive activities are well implemented.

Can we declare victory? Dramatic changes are occurring in the corporate information processing environment. In particular, the entry of the Internet into the business world has resulted in:

- New offerings in traditional businesses

- New views of the customer

- New forms of mergers, such as virtual alliances

- New information sources augmenting that of the corporation's own

While these changes suddenly rendered core systems and data collections (temporarily) less relevant to the leading edge of the business, the reality is that:

- New offerings demand concurrent access to multiple operational systems.

- New views of the customer require access to varied and hitherto unrelated collections of data, augmented by external information sources.

- Virtual alliances call for the connection and integration of the unlike, at times incompatible, operational systems of two or more corporations. Ultimately, the extension of business processes across enterprises is observed through these connections.

The Application Integration pattern

Common among many practical business scenarios is the need to integrate multiple applications, services, and data. Inspecting a number of complex e-business systems, across many industries, certain common Application Integration patterns can be observed. These Application Integration patterns are defined in solutions aimed at integrating multiple applications, information sources, or complete Application patterns. Specifically, these "back-end" Integration patterns are transparent to the user. (This domain of design is also referred to as *Enterprise Application Integration.*)

Access and Application Integration patterns differ from the rest of the patterns in this book in that they do not, by themselves, provide business solutions. Rather, they support the implementation of certain Business patterns, such as many of the Self-Service, Information Aggregation, and Extended Enterprise patterns. In addition, they make Composite business patterns feasible by integrating implementations of two or more Business patterns.

While there are a number of different ways to categorize the Application Integration patterns, one particular aspect stands out: the choice of processes or data as the focus of integration. For each of these two categories, this chapter:

- Examines the fundamental services used by the respective patterns

- Offers a convenient classification for determining their use

- Describes a number of selected patterns

The number of possibilities, considering the range of functions, topologies, and technical implementations, is too large to cover here. We have limited ourselves to some practical examples that are either important to the Business patterns already discussed or may enable Composite patterns. (A more detailed exposition of Application Integration patterns is available from the "Patterns for e-business" Web site.)

Examples of the patterns' usage, the services contained, and their characteristics are given throughout this chapter. As a result, it documents the criteria by which you might evaluate these Application patterns for your own projects.

Process-Focused Application Integration patterns

Process-Focused application integration patterns are observed where multiple automated business processes are combined to yield a new business offering or to provide a consolidated view of some business entity. An often-quoted example is the consolidated view of the state of all relationships of the business with a particular customer.

This mode of integration is highly flexible. In its more sophisticated form, it enables "late binding" of the targets of integration and is particularly useful in tying together different platforms and technologies. However, it represents a more difficult design and development task compared to data-focused integration, and often requires complex middleware. (The term "late binding," in this context, is used to contrast the Process-Focused application integration pattern, where the connection with other applications can be decided after the application has been developed or acquired, with the Data-Focused application integration pattern, where the need for a connection is decided in advance and development proceeds accordingly.)

The description of the Process-Focused application integration patterns in this chapter is organized as follows:

- The common services that make up the various patterns are described.

- Some categorization is suggested, to offer a broader perspective.

- The more significant, practical Application patterns for Application Integration are described.

Common services for the Process-Focused patterns

These Application Integration patterns contain the following well-defined set of services, combinations of which are used in the patterns observed in practice:

- Protocol Adapter

- Message Handler

- Data Transformation

- Decomposition/Recomposition

- Routing/Navigation

- State Management

- Security

- Local Business Logic

- (Business) Unit-of-Work Management

The Protocol Adapter service

Protocol adapters transform the protocol used by a communicating partner application. They are particularly important for allowing integration with legacy systems, since legacy systems typically cannot be changed to adopt a new, common protocol. Instead, legacy systems may require terminal emulators, for example.

Software components, which implement protocols native to an integration hub, are also included in this service. Examples include messaging and IIOP.

The Message Handler service

Message handlers deal with the discovery (parsing) of the in-bound message content, the optional conversion to a common internal format, and the building of the format expected by the target systems. Current implementations use XML as the internal format and, increasingly, also for the out-bound format.

The Data Transformation service

The Data Transformation service frequently references a repository of common data formats to resolve data representation (schema) differences between the applications to be integrated. In simpler cases, this service can be performed by message handlers, especially if you are using the power of XML.

The Decomposition/Recomposition service

One of the main attractions of application integration is the ability to access multiple applications with a single request. To make this possible, a service is required to turn a complex, compound request into a series of simple distinct requests (decomposition), and then to compile the results into a single response (recomposition). This service is particularly important if the source of the request is an end-user.

The Routing/Navigation service

The Routing/Navigation service is also referred to as *micro workflow* or *system workflow*. The multiple requests generated by the Decomposition/Recomposition service can be executed in an arbitrary sequence or with parallelism. The ordering of the execution is sometimes referred to as *message choreography*. Essentially, it represents the navigation among the target systems, driven by business rules. This navigation frequently records the degree of completeness of the request and the cases when error messages must be generated.

In its primitive form, navigation merely performs the routing of a request to the target adapter/connection.

The State Management service

The State Management service is an optional facility supporting the preservation of state information between multiple application message exchanges. It can also support work-in-progress data, obviating the need for repeated access to target systems.

The Security service

Permission to access the participating applications may be associated with the requesting application itself, or this application may carry the credentials of a user initiating the actions. Consequently, access control can be applied as far as the requesting application (a transit of trust) or only from the integration hub (a trusted source) that authenticated the original request.

The Local Business Logic service

The Local Business Logic service provides an opportunity to augment the results of compound requests or, in a more complex case, to generate additional requests. The business logic frequently drives the navigation as well.

The (Business) Unit-of-Work Management service

A number of Application patterns involved in application integration need to execute under transactional control such that a unit of work completes entirely, or not at all. The unit of work here is defined in a broad sense, which may span multiple, independent changes occurring within independent applications, at times during an extended time period.

Categorization of Process-Focused application integration patterns

The Application Integration patterns can be classified according to their functions, mode of connection, or topology.

By functions

The following functions are provided by the integration-enabling middleware:

- Message pass-through or simple connection

- Message routing, in which a single connection can be routed to multiple alternative destinations

- Message enhancement (value-added integration), in which compound requests, controlled by business rules and augmented by local logic and data, are supported

- Managed process (message workflow) integration, in which multi-step business processes comprising "long-running transactions" are supported

Mode of connection

The patterns are classified by the nature of the connection, either synchronous or asynchronous.

Topology

Patterns may be deployed as:

- Point-to-point, where the integration is between two partners, regardless of the number of potential partners in the system

- Multi-point, where the interaction occurs between one initiator and multiple partners

Selected Process-Focused application integration patterns

The Application patterns in this chapter have been included because of their ubiquity or future significance. Although the specific application integration styles used to implement the Process-Focused application integration patterns vary from one industry to another, a survey of such applications in multiple industries reveals certain common approaches that have been successful. In this chapter, such successful approaches are captured by the four Application Integration patterns shown in Figure 12.1.

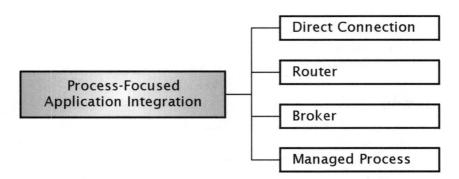

Figure 12.1: These four Process-Focused application integration patterns have been successful in many different industries.

∾ The Direct Connection application pattern

The Direct Connection application pattern helps to structure a system design that allows a pair of applications to communicate directly with each other.

Business and IT drivers

Table 12.1 summarizes the business and IT drivers for this pattern.

Table 12.1: *Business and IT drivers for the Direct Connection application pattern*

Business drivers		IT drivers	
Improve the organizational efficiency.	✓	Leverage existing skills.	✓
Reduce the latency of business events.	✓	Leverage the legacy investment.	✓
Support a structured exchange.	✓	Provide back-end application integration.	✓
Support real-time access to/from applications.	✓	Minimize the application's complexity.	✓
Support the dynamic routing of application "messages."		Minimize the enterprise's complexity.	
Support real-time access to/from business services.			
Support business processes needing long-running transactions.			

The primary business driver for choosing this Application pattern is to enable one application to gain direct and real-time access to another application. The goal is to reduce the latency of business events.

Solution

This pattern offers a simple connection. The mode of connection could be either blocking (synchronous) or non-blocking, and it represents a point-to-point topology. The Protocol Adapter, Message Handler, and Data Transformation services are used.

Figure 12.2 shows the application divided into two logical tiers: application tier 1 and application tier 2. Each of these tiers may represent a new application, a modified existing application, or an unmodified existing application.

Typically, an asynchronous communication mechanism is used for this pattern. The primary reason for choosing asynchronous instead of synchronous communication is to minimize the dependence of the service levels in one application on those of another application. The use of an asynchronous communication mechanism ensures that during a failure, requests can still be sent to the other application to be processed later, while the initiating application can continue its processing without having to wait for the response.

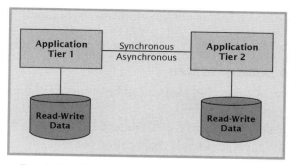

Figure 12.2: The Direct Connection application pattern has two logical tiers.

Predominantly asynchronous Message Oriented Middleware (MOM) such as MQSeries from IBM is used for implementing this Application pattern. The application must use a mutually agreed-upon message format or a mapping to this format provided by a message handler.

Guidelines for use

A direct connection between applications is typically inflexible, in that any changes to one application may have knock-on effects on others. Such changes can be both expensive and time-consuming.

Benefits

Message Oriented Middleware is a key enabler of this Application Integration pattern today. An example of this is MQSeries, whose key features are guaranteed delivery and "once and once only" delivery of messages.

Limitations

The number of connections and the attendant implementation effort and operational complexity grows nonlinearly with the number of applications connected in this way. Also, little reuse is possible.

Because this Application pattern implements a point-to-point interface between the two applications, it cannot be used either for intelligent routing of requests, for decomposition and recomposition of requests, or for invoking complex business process workflow as a result of a request that was received from an application. If those are needed, consider the more advanced Application patterns discussed in this chapter.

Putting the pattern to use

The Direct Connection pattern can be observed in the Extended Enterprise::Exposed Application and the Self-Service::Directly Integrated Single Channel application patterns. Similarly, as introduced in Chapters 5 and 6, Composite patterns frequently incorporate this Application pattern.

～ The Router application pattern

The Router application pattern structures a system design that allows an application "message" to be passed under the control of business rules to another application. This Application pattern can be viewed as a variation on the more general Broker application pattern described next. The latter enables 1:N application connectivity, while the Router application pattern enables only 1:1 application connectivity.

Business and IT drivers

Table 12.2 summarizes the business and IT drivers for this pattern.

The primary business driver for choosing this Application pattern is to increase business flexibility by allowing dynamic message flows that can be easily changed. The primary IT driver is to reduce the large number of interconnections (of N^2 order) to a much smaller number (of $N + N$ order), leading to a significant simplification and cost reduction.

Table 12.2: *Business and IT drivers for the Router application pattern*

Business drivers		IT drivers	
Improve the organizational efficiency.	✓	Leverage existing skills.	✓
Reduce the latency of business events.	✓	Leverage the legacy investment.	✓
Support a structured exchange.	✓	Provide back-end application integration.	✓
Support real-time access to/from applications.	✓	Minimize the application's complexity.	✓
Support the dynamic routing of application "messages."	✓	Minimize the enterprise's complexity.	✓
Support real-time access to/from business services.			
Support business processes needing long-running transactions.			

Solution

This Application pattern provides a routing function to allow any attached (initiating) application using a single router link to connect to one of multiple target applications. The connections can be blocking (synchronous), but in most implementations, they are non-blocking (asynchronous). While access to multiple applications is supported, at any given time, an application is connected to only one other application. Thus the active connection topology is point-to-point. The Protocol Adapter, Message Handler, Data Transformation (optional), Routing, and Security services are used.

Figure 12.3 shows the application divided into three logical tiers:

- The initiating application tier, on the left in Figure 12.3, is the source of the message flow in this pattern.

- Each target application tier, on the right, may represent a new application, a modified existing application, or an unmodified existing application.

- The broker rules tier serves to simplify the proliferation of direct connections. The essence of the integration is still point-to-point, with only two partners participating in a connection at any given time. All partner's roles are equal.

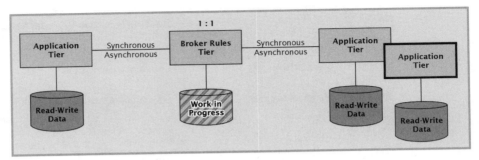

Figure 12.3: The Router application pattern has three logical tiers.

This pattern supports the definition of a common message format, used in the broker, and mapped into the specific formats of the participating applications. Commercial message brokers, such as IBM's MQSeries Integrator, are suitable to implement this pattern.

Guidelines for use

With the intervening (router) component, asynchronous connections are particularly attractive, although synchronous connections are still possible due to the one-to-one connection.

Benefits

This Application pattern may be used to increase the scalability of connections by providing session concentration for access to high-demand applications.

Limitations

This pattern satisfies only elementary integration requirements.

Putting the pattern to use

The Router application pattern can be observed in the Self-Service::Router application pattern.

The Broker application pattern

The Broker application pattern occurs in designs where one application can access other applications through a set of business services that offer a large degree of independence between the initiating application and the target applications.

Business and IT drivers

Table 12.3 summarizes the business and IT drivers for this pattern.

Table 12.3: *Business and IT drivers for the Broker application pattern*

Business drivers		IT drivers	
Improve the organizational efficiency.	✓	Leverage existing skills.	✓
Reduce the latency of business events.	✓	Leverage the legacy investment.	✓
Support a structured exchange.	✓	Provide back-end application integration.	✓
Support real-time access to/from applications.	✓	Minimize the application's complexity.	✓
Support the dynamic routing of application "messages."	✓	Minimize the enterprise's complexity.	✓
Support real-time access to/from business services.	✓		
Support business processes needing long-running transactions.			

The primary business driver for choosing this Application pattern is to increase business flexibility by allowing an application to make a business request that is externally decomposed into multiple distinct messages or requests. Any responses to these multiple requests can then be combined using the appropriate recomposition rules.

Solution

Figure 12.4 shows the application divided into three logical tiers:

- The initiating application tier is the source of the message flow in this Application pattern.

- Each of the target application tiers may represent a new application, a modified existing application or an unmodified existing application.

- The broker rules tier reduces the proliferation of direct connections. In addition, this tier may support message broadcasting, message decomposition/recomposition, and message enhancement by the use of local logic and a local data store. This pattern also supports the definition of a common message format used in the broker and mapped into the specific formats of the participating applications.

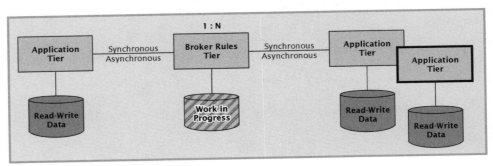

Figure 12.4: The Broker application pattern has three logical tiers.

The Broker application pattern provides far more than simple application integration. Through decomposition and navigation, it enables the implementation of new business functions composed of a number of existing business functions. The mode of connections is predominantly non-blocking. The connection topology, in view of the simultaneous connection to multiple applications, is multi-point. The services used are Protocol Adapter, Message Handler, Data Transformation (optional), Decomposition/Recomposition, Routing, State Management, Security, and Unit-of-Work Management (optional).

The participants' roles are not equal: the initiator (on the left side in Figure 12.4) and the responders (on the right side) are distinguished. This pattern is of particular interest in e-business solutions where the initiator is a Web application server acting on behalf of a user-initiated complex request.

The data transformation may include content as well as format, such as mapping to a common part number in a manufacturing system. Commercial message brokers, such as IBM's MQSeries Integrator (together with a "technology preview" Supportpac IA72 on Windows NT and AIX, which is currently needed to support decomposition/recomposition) are suitable to implement all the features of this Application pattern. Full support of all the features of this pattern is expected in a future product release. The implementation of a business unit-of-work spanning the message flows is possible, although this requires the development of compensating transactions [1] that can restore the data to a state that existed before the change (thus reversing the update).

Guidelines for use

Asynchronous connections are recommended to simplify the customization and operation of the Broker pattern. Care should be exercised if trying to implement unit-of-work control from end to end, as development of compensating transactions can be quite complex.

Benefits

This Application pattern may be used to reduce the overall enterprise application integration complexity, as well as to hide the complexity of back-end systems from a requesting application.

Limitations

Use of this Application pattern increases response time and requires special design considerations. For example, you must avoid introducing a single point of failure when accessing multiple target applications. (This exposure, however, is frequently mitigated by deploying the broker in a clustered configuration.)

Putting the pattern to use

This pattern underlies the Self-Service::Decomposition and Extended Enterprise::Exposed Services application patterns.

The Managed Process application pattern

The Managed Process application pattern provides support for long-running transactions (conversations) that support many business processes, such as insurance claims and quotations.

Business and IT drivers

Table 12.4 summarizes the business and IT drivers for this pattern. The primary business driver for choosing this Application pattern is to increase business flexibility by allowing a business process to be controlled by rules external to the required applications. The rules may also be defined to include compensation mechanisms where earlier actions need to be reversed. These rules may also invoke manual and other processes.

Table 12.4: *Business and IT drivers for the Managed Process application pattern*

Business drivers		IT drivers	
Improve the organizational efficiency.	✓	Leverage existing skills.	✓
Reduce the latency of business events.	✓	Leverage the legacy investment.	✓
Support a structured exchange.	✓	Provide back-end application integration.	✓
Support real-time access to/from applications.	✓	Minimize the application's complexity.	✓
Support the dynamic routing of application "messages."	✓	Minimize the enterprise's complexity.	✓
Support real-time access to/from business services.	✓		
Support business processes needing long-running transactions.	✓		

Solution

The Managed Process application pattern further enhances the value of application integration by extending the Broker pattern's functions with complex navigation and flow logic, essentially implementing a workflow. The other characteristics are unchanged from the Broker pattern. This pattern uses all of the services of the Broker pattern, and adds the Local Business Logic service.

Figure 12.5 shows the application divided into three logical tiers:

- The (optional) initiating application tier is one of the possible sources of the message flow in this pattern. Alternatively, it could be started from such sources as a timer event or a manual action.

- Each of the target application tiers may represent a new application, a modified existing application, or an unmodified existing application.

- The BPM (Business Process Manager) rules tier reduces the proliferation of direct connections.

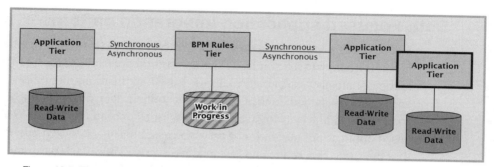

Figure 12.5: The Managed Process application pattern has three logical tiers.

This Application pattern is particularly well-suited to implementing business unit-of-work control across a sequence of manual and automated transactions. High-end commercial message broker products, frequently extended with specialized functions (such as IBM's MQSeries Workflow or WebSphere Business Integrator), are suitable to implement this pattern.

Guidelines for use

It is important to strike the right performance/flexibility balance between task flow among multiple tasks within an application, and workflow external to multiple applications.

Benefits

This Application pattern may be used to flexibly automate complex, long-running business transactions so that the quality of service to the user and the customer can be better managed.

Limitations

Use of this Application pattern may increase individual application response times and produce a single point of failure in accessing multiple target applications.

Putting the pattern to use

This pattern underlies the Extended Enterprise::Managed Public and Private Processes application pattern.

Data-Focused application integration patterns

Data-Focused application integration patterns differ from the Process-Focused group primarily in the timing of the integration decision (early binding) and the mode of data access. In the Process-Focused application integration patterns, all the applications retained control over access to their data, and thus implemented their individual data-access logic and business rules only in one place. With Data-Focused application integration, every interested party accesses the (shared) data—either the same or a replicated instance—directly. Thus, each party must implement its own data access logic for the data to be shared.

These patterns, in general, require less investment in middleware, and the middleware that is used operates at the data store level, and is not exposed to the applications. The advantage of these patterns is their potential for better performance and availability (due to the fewer hops in the path of execution). The disadvantages are that they make data management rather complex, they frequently call upon very substantial development effort, and they offer less flexibility. This approach can also result in the duplication of associated business logic in multiple applications.

The description of the Data-Focused application integration patterns is organized as follows:

- The common services found in these patterns are described.

- Categorization is offered.

- Two of the more significant and practical Application patterns are described.

Common services

The following common services are identified in these patterns:

- Replication/Data Movement

- Cleansing/Transformation

- Augmentation

The Replication/Data Movement service

Data replication is the process of creating a consistent copy of operational data, directly usable by a Data Manager, and thus by an application. (The Data Manager may be a relational database manager such as IBM's Universal Data Base, or a file manager such as Andrews File System. This definition is contrasted with, for example, the creation of an image copy for data recovery purposes.)

The copy can be created by the use of software (data management middleware) or hardware (disk copy), which is controlled by events (such as an update) or by a schedule. The choice of the mode of replication and its frequency requires design trade-offs driven by the need for data currency versus the cost and operational complexity.

The Cleansing/Transformation service

The creation of a new shared, operational copy from multiple data stores often calls for the rationalization of content, both to comply with corporate data standards and to create a single, consistent value for a particular instance of data, such as a customer address. This is achieved through the Data Cleansing and Transformation services, implemented through commercial utilities or custom programming. (Note that the transformation referred to here is very similar to the service described in the Process-Focused application integration.)

The Augmentation service

Frequently, when existing data is being consolidated for new purposes such as integration, it is extended or augmented with additional attributes—either as a superset of all existing attributes or by actually adding a new attribute. This augmentation may also occur (in-line) in the Process-Focused application integration patterns, but it requires custom programming. XML-based techniques promise significant improvements for this service.

Categorization

The Data-Focused application integration patterns form two categories:

- Patterns that enable the distribution of data, creating a local, common view for each of the participant applications

- Patterns that enable the access of a single, consolidated data store

Both patterns are observed and can be deployed in point-to-point or multi-point topologies.

Selected Data-Focused application integration patterns

The following Application patterns have been included because of their ubiquity or future significance. It is important to note that these Application patterns can also be observed in designs that are not intended as integration, such as in new systems.

The specific application integration styles used to implement the Data-Focused application integration patterns varies from one industry to another, but a survey of such applications in multiple industries reveals certain common approaches that have been successful. Two such successful Application patterns, shown in Figure 12.6, are described in the following pages.

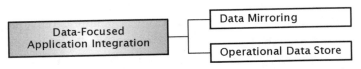

Figure 12.6: These two Data-Focused application integration patterns have been successful in many different industries.

∿ The Data Mirroring application pattern

The Data Mirroring application pattern enables the integration of disparate applications by making a read-only copy of the data available to a partner application. This is a common variant on the Propagation application pattern (included in the more comprehensive list of Application Integration patterns documented on the "Patterns for e-business" Web site).

In this case, no transformation is applied to the source data—it is a simple copy. The middle tier is optional, but is included to allow for multi-point propagation. The population may occur in batch or on an event basis using triggers.

Business and IT drivers

Table 12.5 summarizes the business and IT drivers for this pattern.

Table 12.5: *Business and IT drivers for the Data Mirroring application pattern*

Business drivers		IT drivers	
Improve the organizational efficiency.	✓	Leverage existing skills.	✓
Reduce the latency of business events.	✓	Leverage the legacy investment.	✓
Support a structured exchange.		Provide back-end application integration.	
Support real-time access to/from applications.	✓	Minimize the application's complexity.	
Support the dynamic routing of application "messages."		Minimize the enterprise's complexity.	✓
Support real-time access to/from business services.	✓		
Support business processes needing long-running transactions.			

Solution

The Data Mirroring application pattern is a frequently observed variant of the Propagation application pattern. The difference between the two is that while the Propagation application pattern allows for schema or data-semantic transformations using the transformation rules, the Data Mirroring application pattern populates the target data stores with no changes to the source data. The Data Mirroring application pattern uses the Data Movement service.

The arrows in Figure 12.7 show the data population flow, while the thick lines on the right show the application access flow. The data population function is divided into two logical tiers: the source data derived from the data store maintained by application 1, and the target data stores accessed by applications 2 and 3.

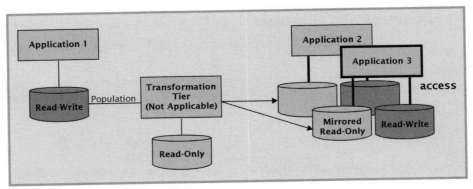

Figure 12.7: This is the Data Mirroring application pattern.

Guidelines for use

Care should be taken when balancing the data currency requirements against the impact on response time, infrastructure costs, and operational complexity.

Benefits

The Data Mirroring application pattern minimizes the changes necessary to existing applications and requires no change to the shared data because of the integration.

Limitations

The "new" applications accessing the shared data have to accept the format and set of attributes implemented by the owning application. The sharing application(s) access the shared data in read-only mode and have to invoke the owning application (via messaging, for example) if changes to the data are required.

Putting the pattern to use

The Data Mirroring application pattern can be used in implementing the Electronic Commerce composite pattern. The catalog may be created by "mirroring" the data from the Content Development System.

The Operational Data Store application pattern

The Operational Data Store pattern is the more complex Data-Focused application integration pattern. It allows an application to access a consolidation of multiple data sources, where each source may be updated and controlled by a separate application. This consolidated data collection frequently represents an improvement over the individual sources in terms of a consistent, enterprise-wide data format and a consistent value (such as a customer number). The data is also augmented to represent the superset of attributes contained in the individual data sources. The "new" applications implement access (usually read-only) to the ODS, which may evolve to become the data-of-record, and thus become a read/write store.

Business and IT drivers

Table 12.6 summarizes the business and IT drivers for this pattern.

Table 12.6: *Business and IT drivers for the Operational Data Store application pattern*

Business drivers		IT drivers	
Improve the organizational efficiency.	✓	Leverage existing skills.	✓
Reduce the latency of business events.	✓	Leverage the legacy investment.	✓
Support a structured exchange.		Provide back-end application integration.	✓
Support real-time access to/from applications.	✓	Minimize the application's complexity.	✓
Support the dynamic routing of application "messages."		Minimize the enterprise's complexity.	✓
Support real-time access to/from business services.	✓		
Support business processes needing long-running transactions.			

Solution

This pattern uses the Data Propagation, Transformation, and (optional) Augmentation services. The arrows in Figure 12.8 show the data population flow in this pattern, while the thick lines above show the potential application access flow.

The data population function is divided into two logical tiers: the source data derived from the data stores maintained by applications 2 through N, and the target data store represented by the ODS. A new or modified application 1 may be provided with read-only access to the ODS. Over time, this may be changed so that a new or modified application (applications 1 through N) may be provided with read/write access to the ODS as this becomes the data-of-record.

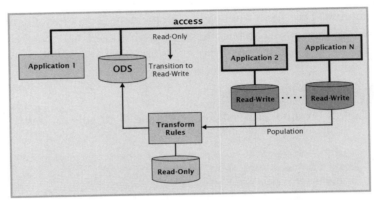

Figure 12.8: This is the Operational Data Store application pattern.

Guidance for use

Access to the ODS from existing applications requires new data-access logic reflecting the new (consolidated) schema. The extent of the new logic increases as the scope of the ODS increases. Similarly, if the intention is to evolve the ODS to become the data-of-record, logic for handling concurrent ODS updates is required.

Benefits

This pattern offers an opportunity to implement more sophisticated applications using enriched corporate data.

Limitations

Substantial effort is required to develop the new data schema and the filters and conversions used to populate the ODS. The benefits of integration need to be balanced against the cost of application changes.

Putting the pattern to use

The ODS is a model underlying the publishing of the consolidated catalog found in the e-Marketplace composite pattern. (The catalog itself is created following the Information Aggregation business pattern.) It can also be found in several

Information Aggregation application patterns and the Self-Service::Agent application pattern.

Step 6f: Identify Application patterns in the FECS solution

Step 4 of the case study, discussed in Chapter 5, identifies the existence of several Application Integration patterns within the FECS solution. A detailed look at the integration requirements of the solution leads to the following five architectural decisions:

1. The order entry function of the solution needs to access the inventory control system on a real-time basis to retrieve the availability of an item and add it to the order, if it is available. This is an example of an Application Integration pattern within a Self-Service business pattern.

2. The order entry function has to integrate with the customer financing function. The financing function will confirm the receipt of the request to the order entry function on a real-time basis.

3. The order entry function has to request customer information from the customer registration function in order to complete the order.

4. The order entry function has to interface to the customer notification function in order to send an e-mail notifying the customer that the order has been completed.

5. The product selection function will need to integrate with the product research forum on an as needed basis. However the integration is not as closely coupled as the inventory control check. This is also not a mission-critical function, although it needs near real-time access.

The first three of these decisions can be implemented using the Application Integration::Direct Connection application pattern. A closer analysis, however, reveals inherent complexities in implementing this integration that may be better handled and implemented using the Application Integration::Broker application pattern.

The integration between the Self-Service business pattern and the Collaboration business pattern requires a direct link between the order entry function and the email notification function. This is best implemented using the Application Integration::Direct Connection application pattern.

The Application Integration::Router application pattern can be used to implement the loosely coupled integration that is required for the fifth item on the list.

These patterns are shown in Figure 12.9.

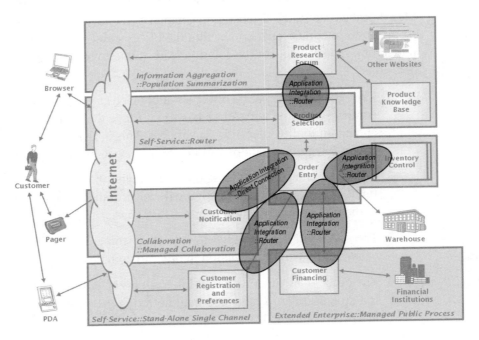

Figure 12.9: Application Integration application patterns are added to the FECS solution.

References

[1]   compensating transactions—Used to restore data to a state that existed before the action causing the change (thus reversing the update).

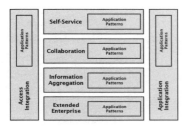

C H A P T E R 13

The next steps
for your organization

Step 7: Summarize all the Application patterns required

Now that the Application patterns have been identified, the resultant Solution Overview Diagram can be completed, as shown in Figure 13.1.

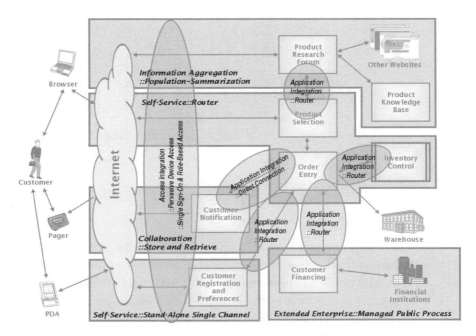

Figure 13.1: With the Application patterns, the FECS solution is complete.

Step 8: Integrate a package into the solution

If there is a preference to use an existing Electronic Commerce package that implements the Electronic Commerce composite pattern, this package will need to integrate with the other Business and Application patterns, as shown in Figure 13.2.

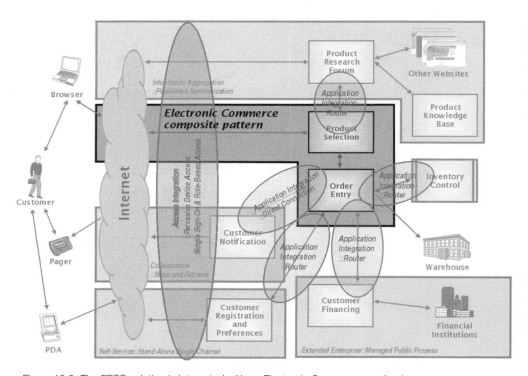

Figure 13.2: The FECS solution is integrated with an Electronic Commerce application.

The next steps

At this point, you have seen an executive's or IT architect's fast path for reusing the Composite, Business, Integration and Application patterns to solve a potentially very complex business problem. (For first-hand evidence describing how others have successfully used the Patterns for e-business to achieve substantial reuse, review the two references on the accompanying CD-ROM. One describes how an IBM customer, Mohawk Industries, benefited from IBM Global Services' use of the Patterns for e-business. The other describes how an IBM business partner,

Foundation Technology Services, used the patterns to achieve 40 percent faster project assessment and 20 percent faster implementation on their client engagements.)

Next, you should hand over this analysis to the lead architect in your organization or a specialist system integrator like IBM Global Services. To achieve a perfect fit with the business requirements, the analysis will have to be extended and completed. Although the lead architect does not have to use the approach and representational style used in this book, it might enable greater executive communication if he or she does.

As part of the more extended analysis, the lead architect will need to implement the following actions:

1. Use a structured development methodology (such as IBM Global Services Method) to ensure:

   a. The full set of business requirements is captured.

   b. A full set of use cases is agreed at the outset.

   c. All development is done within the context of an overall implementation architecture.

   d. The need for availability, scalability, recovery, and other nonfunctional requirements are fully engineered into the recommended physical configuration.

2. Expand the business description to include the full set of business requirements and the multiple use cases that need to be addressed, exploiting the approach used in step 1 of the case study, presented in Chapter 2.

3. Using the business description and the use cases, document the key business functions, predefined processes, and required actors in Use Case Overview Diagrams, exploiting the approach used in step 2 of the case study, also presented in Chapter 2.

4. Using the Solution Overview Diagram as a template, mark up the Use Case Overview Diagram to depict the Business patterns that can be seen within the proposed solution to satisfy each use case, exploiting the approach used in step 3 of the case study, presented in Chapter 4.

5. Extend each Use Case Overview Diagram by drawing ellipses to show the Integration patterns that can be seen, exploiting the approach used in step 4 of the case study, presented in Chapter 5.

6. Review whether a package implementing an existing Composite pattern might be potentially relevant, exploiting the approach used in step 5 of the case study, described in Chapter 6.

7. For each Business and Integration pattern, use the tables of key business and IT drivers and other technical requirements to select the probable best-fit Application pattern, exploiting the approach used in steps 6a through 6f of the case study, described in Chapters 7 through 12.

8. With this understanding of the Application patterns required, determine whether a package implementation of a Composite pattern will meet your overall system integration requirements, exploiting the approach used in steps 7 and 8 of the case study, discussed earlier in this chapter.

9. Before proceeding further, review the next levels of reusable patterns' assets:

   a. Visit the "Patterns for e-business" Web site at http://www.ibm.com/framework/patterns. For each Business and Integration pattern required, navigate to the selected Application pattern, and then review the matching Runtime patterns.

   b. Navigate to the appropriate runtime product based on the preferred platform.

   c. Navigate to the best-practice guidelines and references for implementing these runtime products.

10. The next steps require significant system integration skills. You might need to call in an experienced system integrator, like IBM Global Services.

11. Compose a custom design that will support all the Use Case Overview Diagram requirements (documented in step 5 above) necessary to satisfy the overall solution. (This custom design might, in time, become a Composite pattern if enough organizations share the same requirements and the same solution design.)

12. Create a custom application design based on the Application patterns selected for each Business and Integration pattern.

13. Develop a custom (logical) runtime design necessary to support this custom application design.

14. Match this custom (logical) runtime design against the existing installation runtime product configuration.

15. Select additional (physical) runtime products from step 9b above that are required to implement the custom runtime design.

16. Using step 9c above, customize the combination of best-practice guidelines to fit your design.

17. Exploit the full set of reusable "Patterns for e-business" assets, such as the Web site, Redbooks, reference documentation, and Pattern Development Kit.

You are only at the beginning of a long voyage to discover the benefit that these coarse-grained patterns can achieve. We encourage you to explore the possibilities for increased communication, increased understanding, increased reuse, and increased speed. We think you will be pleasantly surprised.

We encourage you to take the journey!

C H A P T E R **14**

e-Marketplace case study

The Retailer's Mega Exchange: A case study

The FutureStep Electronics case study has been used throughout this book to illustrate how you can use the Patterns for e-business during the early stages of the application development life cycle to reduce risk and improve the time to market. To summarize this methodology in a single chapter, we present the Retailer's Mega Exchange case study.

Understanding e-Marketplaces

Before focusing on the case study, it is important to establish a common understanding of e-Marketplaces. We define an e-Marketplace as an electronic gathering place that brings together multiple buyers and sellers, and facilitates buying and selling between them. In these marketplaces, a market maker seeks to control the point of commerce by creating marketplace liquidity and providing a value-added trading alternative to buyers and sellers. Figure 14.1 provides a conceptual view of an e-Marketplace.

In this environment, buyers benefit by being able to access

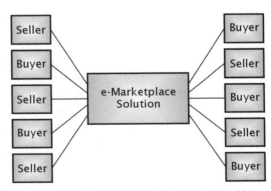

Figure 14.1: This is a conceptual view of an e-Marketplace.

product-specific information and by taking advantage of lower prices from competing suppliers. Sellers get a new, efficient distribution channel to new markets and the opportunity to compete with previously entrenched vendors. In short, e-Marketplaces facilitate product availability, increase price leverage, and improve service levels due to the competitive forces present in a consolidated, frictionless market.

At the highest level, e-Marketplaces can be segmented into two types:

- *Horizontal e-Marketplaces* typically focus on reducing the inefficiencies of spot purchasing. They address expenditures that are applicable across a wide range of industries, such as office supplies, business services, or temporary employees. The primary value proposition of a horizontal e-Marketplace is the delivery of goods and services at reduced prices.

- *Vertical e-Marketplaces* facilitate the exchange of manufactured inputs to specific industries or segments, utilizing the Internet's connectivity to eliminate an industry's "pain points." For example, a vertical marketplace for computer manufacturers might cover printed circuit boards, memory chips, and other integrated circuit chips.

  Vertical e-Marketplaces enter an industry's supply chain and add value by efficiently managing interactions between industry buyers and sellers. They offer advantages for both systematic and spot transactions. The vertical e-Marketplace's model is currently receiving the greater amount of attention.

Three basic trading models currently exist in the e-Marketplace:

- *Aggregators* facilitate trade by consolidating multiple suppliers in a single location. With a searchable catalog of supplier product information in a common format, buyers can efficiently select products with real-time pricing, product descriptions, and comparisons at a single point of contact. The aggregator model is the simplest of the three models, and is therefore the most commonly adopted. It is also the model that companies are most comfortable with because of its product breadth and static pricing mechanism.

- *Auctions* are used to unload surplus products and increase inventory turnover. They focus on delivering goods or services to buyers at reduced prices and creating a controlled competitive buying venue that quickly liquidates excess or used equipment. A seller often initiates auctions, and buyers bid their best offers in the anticipation of acquiring the goods being auctioned. The highest bidding buyer wins the auction.

Reverse auctions, on the other hand, are initiated by buyers. Here, buyers invite best bids from sellers who wish to fulfill the buyer's needs. The lowest bidding seller wins the reverse auction. e-Marketplaces implement several variations on this type of auction, including the English reverse auction, the Dutch reverse auction, and the Japanese reverse auction.

- *Exchanges* provide trading rules and historic pricing to enable fast trading by matching bid-ask offers and pricing in real time. Exchanges are the most complicated of the transaction models.

The e-Marketplace is created and maintained by a "market maker" who brings the buyers and suppliers together. The market maker assumes the responsibility of the e-Marketplace administration and performs maintenance tasks to ensure that the e-Marketplace is open for business.

A market maker's primary purpose is to bring together a target audience of corporate buyers and sellers to solve specific industry problems embedded in the trading process. Market makers provide solutions that go beyond the first wave of B2B e-commerce, to provide dynamic, open e-Marketplaces that can enter the supply chain of vertical and horizontal industries, introducing new ways of buying and selling.

The various business services provided by a mature e-Marketplace, as shown in Figure 14.2, are as follows:

- The Community and Collaboration service facilitates various types of collaborations between the members of the community. Such collaborations are often undertaken for supply chain management, product design, and sourcing purposes, and for demand planning.

- The Dynamic Trade service facilitates the execution of the various trading models, such as an aggregated catalog, auctions, reverse auctions, RFP/RFQ, and exchange.

- The Content service is responsible for the population and maintenance of various types of contents, including aggregated catalogs, industry news, and contracts. Business intelligence and data mining techniques are used to analyze the content and distill meaningful information from this vast amount of data that can provide the insight required to create a sustainable competitive advantage.

- The Transaction service deals with order management, fulfillment, logistics management, financing, and invoicing.

- The Marketplace Administration service deals with user and member registration, security, auditing, and exception handling.

These services run on top of the e-Marketplace infrastructure, which is typically hosted by a third-party service provider with specific expertise in managing large e-business infrastructures, so that the quality of service required by an e-Marketplace can be guaranteed. Finally, a global e-business backbone connects this e-Marketplace with external service providers such as other marketplaces, content providers, transportation companies, and financial institutions.

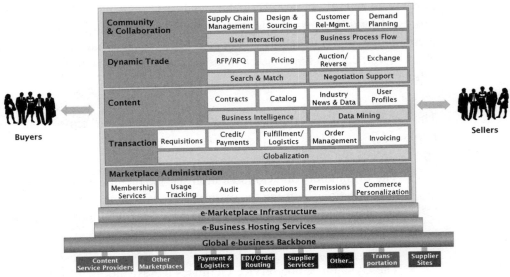

Figure 14.2: Various business services are provided by a mature e-Marketplace.

While a detailed description of e-Marketplaces is beyond the scope of this book, this explanation is sufficient to continue the case study with a common understanding. From this brief description of e-Marketplaces, it is evident that B2B solutions represent some of the most comprehensive and complex e-business applications today.

The case study

The Retailers' Mega Exchange (RME) is a new company established to create an e-Marketplace to enable retailers and their suppliers to trade electronically. During the first release of this e-Marketplace, RME wishes to provide the following functionality to its end-users:

- Content:
  - Retail industry news
  - An aggregated catalog from multiple suppliers
- Trading:
  - Search and select
  - Auction and reverse auction
- Transaction:
  - Order management
- Community and collaboration:
  - Personalized user interaction
  - Purchase-order authorization workflow
  - E-mail and chat facilities

To achieve RME's time-to-market needs for the first release, it would like to limit the access channel to the Web browser. However, it wants to keep the architecture open, so other access channels such as mobile devices and voice response units (VRUs) can be supported in the future.

Notice that many areas of the case study have been simplified by not including key topics such as external catalog search, supply chain management, demand planning, credit and payment, fulfillment and logistics, invoicing, data mining, and business intelligence. We have done this to facilitate the discussion and keep it focused on explaining the concept of the Patterns for e-business.

Step 1: Develop a high-level business description

In the first step of the solution definition process, the business owner should develop a high-level business description that illustrates the core business functions of the proposed solution. This description need not be any more sophisticated than one or two clearly worded paragraphs describing the actors who participate in the solution and the high-level interactions between these actors that explain the core business functions.

The actors represent entities that exist outside the scope of the solution, but are critical for its completeness. For example, actors can be people, devices, external institutions, legacy applications that will not be modified by this solution, and packaged applications with which this solution will interact. To better understand this concept, consider the following business description developed for the RME solution. (The underlined items identify the actors in the solution. The items in **bold** represent the high-level business functions that need to be provided by the solution.)

> The RME first release will provide a set of e-Marketplace services for trading partners, who are retailers buying on this exchange and suppliers selling on this exchange. The RME solution will be browser-based and will be accessible across the Internet by our end-users.

> The RME system will provide **marketplace administration** services to retailers and suppliers. This service will allow them to register their company names, locations, the types of services they expect to leverage from this e-Marketplace, the lists of users from their organization who can trade on the exchange, and the permission levels of the users.

> The **retail industry news** will be aggregated from multiple news content providers. This service will provide users with a one-stop shop for key trends in the retail industry that they can use to make informed buying and selling decisions.

The **aggregated catalog** will consolidate items from multiple suppliers using a common format. This catalog will be kept updated by receiving feeds from the supplier's catalogs on an ongoing basis.

A retailer who wishes to buy a certain item can **search** the aggregated catalog, compare products from multiple suppliers, and **select** the best product. Alternatively, the retailer can initiate a **reverse auction** for that item, inviting suppliers to bid their lowest offer for the item. Conversely, the retailer can bid in an **auction** for that item initiated by a supplier, if one is already in progress.

Using one or more of the above options, once the buyer decides to buy a set of products from a supplier, he or she can then initiate a purchase order for those items using the **order management** component. This component electronically sends purchase orders to the supplier's order processing system. A copy of the purchase order is also sent to the retailer's purchasing system. This **order management** component tracks the order to its completion by facilitating all related communications between the supplier's order management system and the retailer's purchasing system.

During this trading experience, end-users can collaborate with one another using **chat** and **e-mail** facilities. In addition, e-mail notification will be used to manage purchase order **authorization workflows**. This functionality is invoked when an end-user places a purchase order that requires authorization from a senior manager before it can be processed. Once the senior manager approves the order, it is electronically processed by the **order management** component.

Finally, the RME system should enable a single sign-on capability across all the business functions. It should also provide a role-based, personalized user interface using the explicit user profile entered during the user's registration.

This short business description captures the high-level requirements for this case study.

Step 2: Develop a Solution Overview Diagram

The next step is to develop a Solution Overview Diagram (SOD) that helps translate the text provided by the business description into a pictorial representation. Once again, the objective is to keep the diagram simple and informative. As mentioned in Chapter 3, four major symbols are used:

- A rectangle representing a high-level business function

- A rectangle with two vertical lines representing one of the actors—an application or package that will interface with the solution but will not be modified or changed by this solution

- A picture or other icon representing the other actors

- A connector that links the other three symbols

The Solution Overview Diagram can be drawn in a few simple stages. The first stage is to analyze the business description developed in the previous step and draw rectangles to represent the key business functions (the items that are bold in the description). For instance, from the business description, the following functions can be identified in the RME system:

- Marketplace administration

- Retail industry news

- Aggregated catalog

- Search and select

- Auctions and reverse auctions

- Order management

- Chat and e-mail

- Authorization workflow

The second stage is to represent any predefined processes (such as external applications or packages that will not be modified by the solution but will interact with it) using a rectangle with two vertical lines. They are:

- The supplier's catalogs

- The supplier's order processing system

- The retailer's purchasing system

The third stage is to use pictures or icons to represent all the remaining actors in the business description. These include:

- News content providers

- Suppliers

- Retailers

- The browser

- The Internet

The resultant diagram is shown in Figure 14.3.

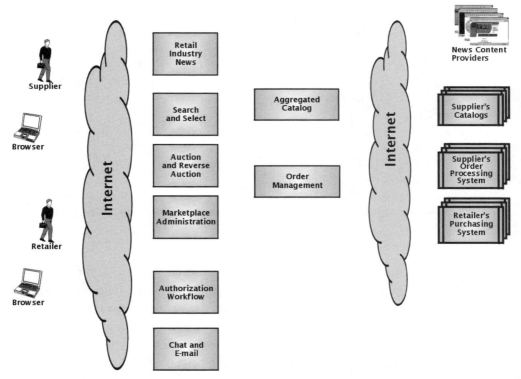

Figure 14.3: The Solution Overview Diagram begins with a display of business functions and actors.

The last stage is to use the business description to walk through each process and link the individual symbols using connectors. This should produce the completed Solution Overview Diagram in Figure 14.4.

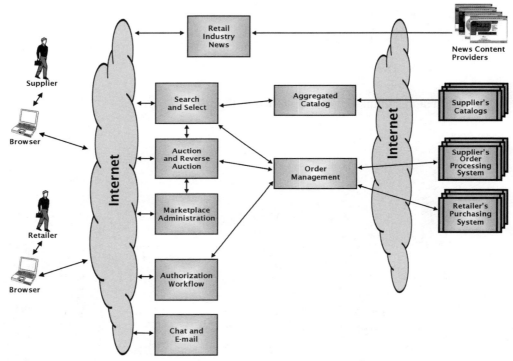

Figure 14.4: With business functions, actors, and connectors, the RME SOD is ready to have patterns applied.

The Solution Overview Diagram provides a concise and comprehensive way of representing the key aspects of the proposed solution. It provides the foundation for the process of identifying and applying the Patterns for e-business.

Step 3: Identify Business patterns

Looking closely at the Solution Outline Diagram in Figure 14.4 with the knowledge of Business patterns and their characteristics, you can observe the following Business patterns in the solution:

- Buyers may search and select items from the aggregated catalog and may place orders for selected items. Users may participate in auctions, reverse auctions, or marketplace administration. These functions involve direct interaction between users, back-end systems (order management), and databases (the aggregated catalog). These interactions indicate a Self-Service business pattern.

- The RME system uses e-mail notifications to initiate authorization workflow when senior management approval is required to complete a purchase order. Similarly, the RME solution provides e-mail and chat facility to enable communication between trading partners. These interactions form two Collaboration business patterns.

- The RME solution aggregates retail industry news from multiple content-provider sites. Similarly, the RME catalog is built by consolidating product data from multiple suppliers. In essence, these two functions focus on the process of taking large volumes of data and extracting meaningful information from them; in other words, they are Information Aggregation business patterns.

- The RME solution must send purchase orders to suppliers for further processing of orders and fulfillment. A copy of the purchase order must also be sent to the retailer who placed the order on the exchange, to notify its legacy accounting systems of the purchase. Copies of the suppliers' catalogs must also be transmitted to the RME site. These functions represent interactions between business processes in separate enterprises, so they form two Extended Enterprise business patterns.

The business or IT executive can create a list that represents the Business patterns occurring in the solution. For the RME solution, this diagram is shown in Figure 14.5.

The executive can also mark up the Solution Overview Diagram to depict the

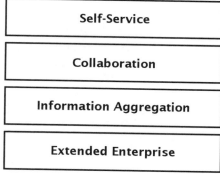

Figure 14.5: This is the pattern diagram for the RME e-Marketplace.

Business patterns existing in the solution. Figure 14.6 uses shaded boxes to identify the Business patterns in the RME solution.

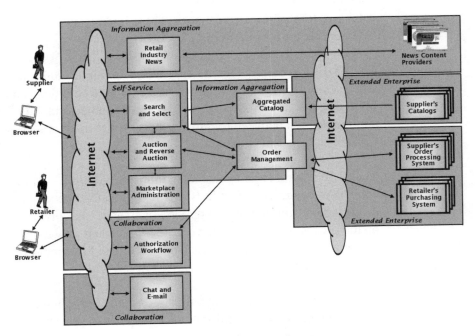

Figure 14.6: Step 3 applies Business patterns to the Solution Overview Diagram.

Step 4: Identify Integration patterns

In step 4, you should first look at each of the lines between the functions and determine how the integration will be accomplished. In most cases, it will be done using the Application Integration pattern. If functions need to be tied together to provide a consistent experience to the user, then an Access Integration pattern is indicated.

Taking a closer look at the Solution Overview Diagram, you can observe Application Integration patterns that link:

- The search and select function to the aggregated catalog function

- The order management function to the authorization workflow function

We have not listed the occurrence of Application Integration patterns within the construct of a specific Business pattern, such as the connectivity between search and select, auction and reverse auction, marketplace administration, and order management. This is because we assume that these functions are part of the same application and hence will communicate with one another through some inter-program communication mechanism (like a subroutine call).

Similarly, the SOD does not show an Application Integration pattern for connectivity between the Extended Enterprise business pattern (describing the interaction between the order management function and the supplier/retailer systems) and the Self-Service business pattern (describing the interaction between users and the search and select, auction and reverse auction, order management, and marketplace admin functions). This is because the order management function here acts as the common component that participates in both these Business patterns. Inside this component, the integration between the sub-components that automate the Extended Enterprise business pattern and the Self-Service business pattern is assumed to be implemented through some inter-program communication mechanism (like a subroutine call). The same observation can be made about the connectivity between the aggregated catalog function and the supplier's catalogs.

There is also a need for an Access Integration pattern that can implement the RME portal functionality to:

- Provide users a seamless and consistent experience that includes a universal sign-on function

- Deliver a role-based, personalized user interface to end-users

The final solution can now be composed by adding these Integration patterns to the list of Business patterns identified in the previous step. This updated diagram for RME is shown in Figure 14.7.

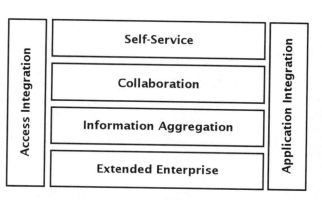

Figure 14.7: This is the pattern diagram for a custom design of the RME solution.

The Solution Overview Diagram can be extended by drawing ellipses to show the Integration patterns. The resultant diagram is shown in Figure 14.8. This diagram will be refined further during the solution development process by breaking the Business and Integration patterns down into their appropriate Application patterns.

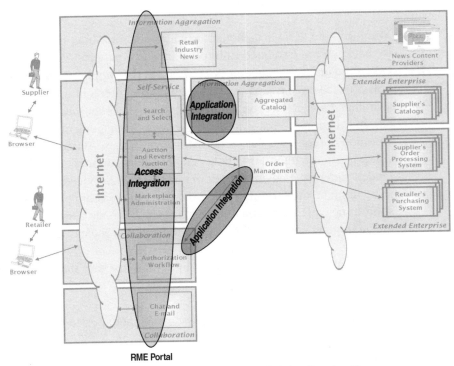

Figure 14.8: Step 4 applies Integration patterns to the Solution Overview Diagram.

Step 5: Identify Composite patterns

You can now look at the Solution Overview Diagram to identify the Composite patterns that occur in the solution. This step is very useful when the executives responsible for this solution wish to implement major portions of its business functions using one or more software packages.

We believe that it is important for designers to go through all the steps of this process, even if the solution will be implemented using vendor packages. This will help define the Application and Runtime patterns that will provide the service-level characteristics (availability, scalability, performance, and so on) expected from the solution. It will also help the executives make informed decisions and have reasonable service level expectations for the chosen packages.

A detailed look at the Solution Overview Diagram and Chapter 6 reveals that major portions of the RME solution can be assembled using the e-Marketplace composite pattern shown in Figure 14.9.

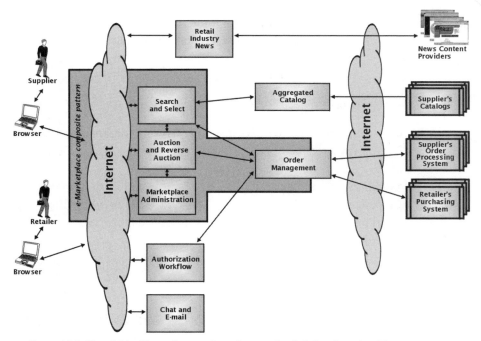

Figure 14.9: Step 5 identifies a Composite pattern on the Solution Overview Diagram.

Based on this Composite pattern, you can assume that the solution may need to use an e-Marketplace package such as WebSphere Commerce Suite, Marketplace Edition or Ariba Marketplace to implement the auction function.

Note that the Composite pattern in Figure 14.9 does not address all the functional needs described in the business description developed in step 1. For example, this Composite pattern does not address the retail industry news and the aggregated catalog requirements. To address these gaps and ensure that the integrated solution can provide the expected level of service, we recommend that the solution be refined further using the subsequent steps before a final product decision is made.

Step 6a: Identify Application patterns for Self-Service

Step 3 of this process identified the existence of a Self-Service business pattern within the RME solution. This is seen when end-users access the search and select, auction and reverse auction, order management, and marketplace admin functions. A detailed look at the requirements of the solution shows the following:

- Once the buyer has chosen the product to buy, either through the search and select, or auction/reverse auction mechanism, the order management component must decompose this request and notify both retailers and suppliers about the purchase order.

- There is a need for intelligent routing and transformation of messages.

- The first release of RME will focus only on one access channel, the Web browser.

Matching these requirements to the business and IT drivers of the various Application patterns for Self-Service, the Self-Service::Decomposition application pattern would be required to automate this Business pattern. Note, however, that the first implementation does not take advantage of all the features provided by the Decomposition application pattern, such as integration across multiple delivery channels. However, it positions RME to support other delivery channels in the future.

Step 6b: Identify Application patterns for Collaboration

Step 3 of this process identified the authorization workflow and chat and e-mail functions as Collaboration business patterns. A closer look at the requirements for the authorization workflow function of the RME solution shows the following:

- There are two-way communications with the users.

- Users are automatically notified when certain events occur within the solution. For instance, an e-mail is sent to the approver as soon as a purchase order is entered that requires authorization before it can be processed.

- If the order is not approved, the originator of the purchase order is notified so that he or she can take the appropriate action.

Based on these requirements, the solution will need to have the following components:

- The clients will need the ability to operate in both a network connected and disconnected mode.

- The server should be able to:

  - Support two-way communication with clients.

  - Send messages to clients triggered by dynamic events within the solution.

  - Route messages to individual functions based on the content of the message.

Based on these requirements, it is clear that the appropriate Application pattern to automate authorization workflow is the Collaboration::Managed Collaboration application pattern.

A similar analysis of chat functionality reveals that it can be automated by the Collaboration::Directed Collaboration application pattern. An analysis of e-mail functionality reveals that it can be automated by the Collaboration::Store and Retrieve application pattern.

Step 6c: Identify Application patterns for Information Aggregation

Earlier, you saw that the Information Aggregation business pattern could be observed in the retail industry news and the aggregated catalog functions of the RME solution. A closer look at the requirements for the retail industry news function of the solution shows the following:

- It distills meaningful information from unstructured data.

- It periodically accesses relevant public and private Web sites to discover information related to the retail industry.

- This discovery process must be limited to a set of authorized content-provider sites.

- The result of the search needs to be summarized to make it more useful to the user who has asked for this data.

Matching these requirements to the various business and IT drivers of the Application patterns for Information Aggregation, the Information Aggregation::Population–Summarization application pattern can be identified as the best fit for the retail industry news population function. The Information Aggregation::Information Access–Read-Only application pattern could provide access to this aggregated and distilled retail industry information.

A similar analysis of the aggregated catalog population function reveals that it can be automated by the Information Aggregation::Population–Multi-Step application pattern. You might notice from the Solution Outline Diagram that the information access in this case is provided by a search and select function, which is automated by an Application pattern for Self-Service. Here, the connectivity between the population and information access function is enabled by a data-focused Application Integration pattern.

Step 6d: Identify Application patterns for Extended Enterprise

Earlier, you saw that the links between the order management function, the supplier's order processing system, and the retailer's purchasing system, as well as the links between the suppliers' catalog and the aggregated catalog, exhibit the Extended Enterprise business pattern. A closer look at this connectivity with suppliers and retailers brings out a few key requirements:

- The machine-to-machine interface provided between the RME systems and the retailer and supplier systems will be conducted over the Internet using an XML data format for information exchange. A strategic decision has been made not to support EDI formats over the VAN for such integration.

- The interaction between the RME solution and suppliers is codified using a Trading Partner Agreement (TPA) established between the Retailers' Mega Exchange and the suppliers. This also applies to the interaction between RME and the retailers.

- The e-Marketplace publishes standard application programming interfaces (APIs) that are used by trading partners to integrate with the exchange.

- These APIs can be accessed using the Simple Object Access Protocol (SOAP) across a secure HTTP connection.

- There is a need to support real-time access to business services provided by the e-Marketplace for trading partners.

- There is a need to support shared business process flows with multiple partners.

Based on these requirements, it is clear that the Extended Enterprise::Managed Public Process application pattern is the best fit for this solution to automate the integration with suppliers and retailers. It can automate all the Extended Enterprise scenarios identified.

Step 6e: Identify Application patterns for Access Integration

Earlier, you saw the need for an Access Integration pattern to provide a single sign-on and provide a role-based, personalized user interface for end-users. A closer look at these requirements brings out a few key issues:

- There is a need to provide a single sign-on across multiple functions that automate different Business patterns, such as Self-Service, Collaboration, and Information Aggregation

- Based on the user role, RME may provide different privileges. For example, only purchasing managers who belong to the retailer (buyer) organization may initiate reverse auctions. Similarly, only supplier (seller) brand managers can initiate an excess inventory auction. Only purchasing managers of the end-product manufacturing company can authorize orders exceeding certain preset limits. This requires role-based access to certain functions across multiple applications such as search and select, auctions and reverse auctions, and authorization workflow.

Matching these requirements to the business and IT drivers table for the Application patterns for Access Integration, it is clear that the Access Integration::Single Sign-On and Role-Based Access application pattern is the best fit to provide the RME portal functionality. In other words, this solution takes advantage of the Security and Administration service, the Presentation service, and the Personalization service.

Recall from Chapter 11 that the best practice for achieving these goals is to externalize the user profile (authentication and authorization information) from individual applications. Here, this goal can be achieved by ensuring that the marketplace administrator creates and maintains such an external centralized user profile. Subsequently, individual applications such as retail industry news, search and select, and authorization workflow need to be designed and configured to access this external, centralized user profile for authentication and authorization purposes.

Step 6f: Identify Application patterns for Application Integration

Earlier, you saw the need for Application Integration patterns to connect the search and select function to the aggregated catalog, and to connect the authorization workflow to the order management function. A closer look at the connectivity between search and select and the aggregated catalog brings out a few key requirements:

- The aggregated catalog is updated periodically by consolidating multiple supplier catalogs on a weekly basis.

- A read-only copy of this catalog must be made available to the search and select tool.

Based on these requirements, it is clear that the data-focused Application Integration::Data Mirroring application pattern is the best fit. A similar analysis of the connectivity between order management and the authorization workflow reveals that messages must be passed between these two components under the control of business rules. The Application Integration::Router application pattern is the ideal one to meet these requirements.

Step 7: Summarize all the Application patterns required

Now that the Application patterns have been identified, the resultant SOD can be completed, as shown in Figure 14.10.

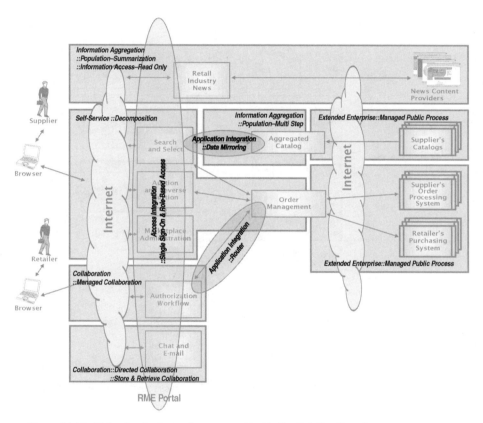

Figure 14.10: All the Application patterns are added to the Solution Overview Diagram.

Step 8: Integrate a package into the solution

If there is a preference to use an existing e-Marketplace package that implements the e-Marketplace composite pattern, it will be necessary to integrate with the other Business and Application patterns. Note that in the case of an e-Marketplace composite pattern, you can no longer assume that the order management function provides the integration between the sub-components that automate the Extended

Enterprise business pattern and the Self-Service business pattern through some inter-program communication mechanism (like a subroutine call). Hence, an additional Application Integration::Router application pattern needs to be included. The resultant diagram is shown in Figure 14.11.

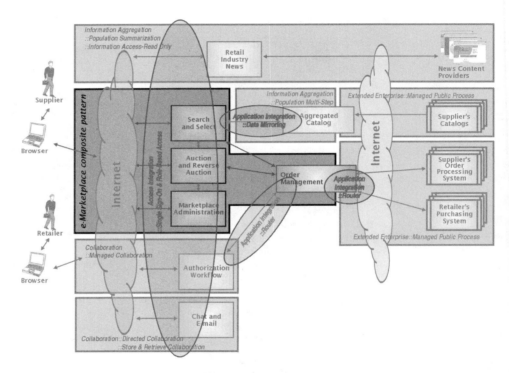

Figure 14.11: When using an e-Marketplace package, an additional Application Integration pattern is required.

About the CD-ROM

This CD-ROM does not install anything on your computer. Simply insert it, and you will automatically be presented with a menu of segments to view or listen to. (You may wish to adjust the volume on your machine before playing the video or audio segments.)

Here is a list of the CD contents:

- The Patterns for e-business demonstration and tutorial.

- Independent analyst reports by Bloor Research (Patterns–BloorReport.pdf) and Butler Group (Patterns–ButlerReport.pdf).

- Customer/business partner videos:
    - Foundation Technology Services cuts time and risk with IBM Patterns for e-business (foundtech.mpg).
    - Mohawk Industries keeps its customers covered with e-business solutions from IBM (Mohpatt.mpg).

- Customer/business partner references:
    - Mohawk Industries keeps its customers covered with e-business solutions from IBM (Patterns_Mohawk.pdf).
    - Foundation Technology Services cuts time and risk with IBM Patterns (Patterns_Foundation_Technologies.pdf).
    - Degussa-Hüls divisions go to market with IBM e-business solutions (Patterns_Degussa_Huls.pdf).

- The IBM Redbooks series on Patterns for e-business:
  - Patterns for e-business: User-to-Business Patterns for Topology 1 and 2 using WebSphere Advanced Edition, SG24-5864-00 (sg245864.pdf)
  - User-to-Business Patterns Using WebSphere Enterprise Edition: Patterns for e-business Series, SG24-6151-00 (sg246151.pdf)
  - User-to-Business Patterns Using WebSphere Advanced and MQSI: Patterns for e-business Series, SG24-6160-00 (sg246160.pdf)
  - Business-to-Business Integration Using MQSeries and MQSI, Patterns for e-business Series, SG24-6010-00 (sg246010.pdf)
  - e-Commerce Patterns Using WebSphere Commerce Suite, Patterns for e-business Series, SG24-6156-00 (sg246156.pdf)
  - e-Marketplace Pattern using WebSphere Commerce Suite, MarketPlace Edition Patterns for e-business Series, SG24-6158-00 (sg246158.pdf)
  - Design and Implement Servlets, JSPs, and EJBs for IBM WebSphere Application Server, SG24-5754-00 (sg245754.pdf)
  - CCF Connectors and Database Connections Using WebSphere Advanced Edition Connecting Enterprise Information Systems to the Web, SG24-5514-00 (sg245514.pdf)
  - User-to-Business Patterns for e-business: Developing AS/400e e-business Applications, SG24-5999-00 (sg245999.pdf)
  - User-to-Business Pattern Using WebSphere Personalization, Patterns for e-business series, SG24-6213-00 (sg246213.pdf)
  - Business Process Management using MQSeries and Partner Agreement Manager, SG24-6166-00 (sg246166.pdf)
  - Integrating WebSphere Commerce Suite With a Back-End Order Management Application, REDP0514 (redp0514.pdf)
  - Connect for iSeries with WebSphere Commerce Suite: BtoB Enabling a WebSphere Commerce Suite Web Site, REDP0127 (redp0127.pdf).
- A direct link to Patterns for e-business resources on the Web at http://www.ibm.com/developerworks/patterns/library/index.html.
- A direct link to the "Patterns for e-business" Web site at http://www.ibm.com/framework/patterns/.

Resources

Links to all of the following pattern resources can be found at
http://www.ibm.com/developerworks/patterns/library/index.html or, where indicated, on this book's CD-ROM.

Customer references (on the book's CD-ROM)

Degussa-Hüls divisions go to market with IBM e-business solutions.

Foundation Technology Services cuts time and risk with IBM Patterns.

Mohawk Industries keeps its customers covered with e-business solutions from IBM.

IBM Redbooks/Redpapers (on the book's CD-ROM)

Business-to-Business Integration Using MQSeries and MQSI, Patterns for e-business Series, SG24-6010-00.

Business Process Management using MQSeries and Partner Agreement Manager, SG24-6166-00

CCF Connectors and Database Connections Using WebSphere Advanced Edition Connecting Enterprise Information Systems to the Web, SG24-5514-00.

Connect for iSeries with WebSphere Commerce Suite: BtoB Enabling a WebSphere Commerce Suite Web Site, REDP0127

Design and Implement Servlets, JSPs, and EJBs for IBM WebSphere Application Server, SG24-5754-00.

e-Commerce Patterns Using WebSphere Commerce Suite, Patterns for e-business Series, SG24-6156-00.

e-Marketplace Pattern using WebSphere Commerce Suite, MarketPlace Edition: Patterns for e-business Series, SG24-6158-00.

Integrating WebSphere Commerce Suite With a Back-End Order Management Application, REDP0514

Patterns for e-business: User-to-Business Patterns for Topology 1 and 2 using WebSphere Advanced Edition, SG24-5864-00. (This is on the book's CD)

Servlet and JSP Programming with IBM WebSphere Studio and VisualAge for Java, SG24-5755-00.

User-to-Business Patterns for e-business: Developing AS/400e e-business Applications, SG24-5999-00

User-to-Business Patterns Using WebSphere Advanced and MQSI: Patterns for e-business Series, SG24-6160-00.

User-to-Business Patterns Using WebSphere Enterprise Edition: Patterns for e-business Series, SG24-6151-00.

User-to-Business Pattern Using WebSphere Personalization, Patterns for e-business series, SG24-6213-00

Independent analyst reports

Bloor Research's review of the IBM Patterns for e-business (PDF file on the book's CD-ROM)

Butler Group's assessment of the IBM Patterns for e-business (PDF file on the book's CD-ROM)

Component Developer Strategies review of the IBM Patterns for e-business(PDF file)

Lotus ScreenCams

Reducing risk by reusing proven assets, Vols. 1 and 2

Patterns Demo

The "Patterns for e-business" demonstration and tutorial is on the book's CD-ROM.

Patterns Development Kit

Patterns Development Kit Lite (PDK Lite)

White papers

Anytime, anywhere access to any information

Design for performance

Design for scalability: IBM high-volume Web site team

Patterns for e-business: Lessons learned from building successful e-business applications

Pervasive computing and the Patterns for e-business

Planning for growth: A proven methodology for capacity planning

The WebSphere software platform

Web site personalization

Glossary

Access Integration pattern

Describes those recurring designs that enable access to one or more Business patterns.

ACID

An acronym for the four primary attributes ensured to any transaction by a transaction monitor: atomicity, consistency, isolation, and durability. The ACID concept is described in ISO/IEC 10026-1:1992, section 4.

Agent application pattern

Structures an application design that provides a unified customer-centric view that can be exploited for mass customization of services and for cross-selling.

Application Integration patterns

Typically observed in solutions that call for the integration of Web-based solutions to core business systems and databases.

Application patterns

Help to refine Business patterns so they can be implemented as computer-based solutions.

Application Programming Interface (API)

Defines how programmers use a particular feature provided by an application.

As-Is Host application pattern

Provides wider intranet access to existing host applications.

authentication

The process of determining whether someone or something is, in fact, who or what it is declared to be. In private and public computer networks (including the Internet), authentication is commonly done through the use of sign-on passwords. Knowledge of the password is assumed to guarantee that the user is authentic.

authorization

The process of giving someone permission to do or have something. A system administrator defines which users are allowed access to the system and what use privileges they are given (such as access to which file directories, hours of access, and amount of allocated storage space). Logically, authorization is preceded by authentication.

best practices

The design, development, deployment and management guidelines for building an application based on a set of nested patterns. These guidelines may be generic to a family of middleware products (with some variations), generic to an industry standard set of technologies (with some vendor variations), or specific to a product or product family.

Broker application pattern

Occurs in designs where one application can access other applications through a set of business services that offer a large degree of independence between the initiating application and the target applications.

Business Data Warehouse (BDW)

A data store containing detailed, reconciled, and historical data, structured according to an enterprise data model and designed to be the single, consistent source for all management information. This data source is seldom accessed by end-users, and then only in a read-only format.

Business Intelligence (BI) applications

Typically focus on internal users, such as executives, managers, and business analysts.

Business patterns

High-level constructs that can be used to establish the primary business purpose of any solution.

Cascading Style Sheets (CSS)

A simple mechanism for adding presentation style to Web documents.

client

The requesting program in a client/server model. For example, a browser is a client that requests services from a Web server.

Collaboration business pattern

Can be observed in e-business solutions that allow users to communicate and share data and information with other users or groups of users on the network.

Common Object Request Broker Architecture (CORBA)

An architecture and specification for creating, distributing, and managing distributed program objects in a network. It allows programs at different locations and developed by different vendors to communicate in a network through an "interface broker." CORBA was developed by a consortium of vendors through the Object Management Group (OMG). It currently includes over 500 member companies.

compensating transactions

Used to restore data to a state that existed before the action causing the change (thus reversing the update).

Customer Relationship Management (CRM)

The essential business process that encompasses an organization's end-to-end engagement with its customers over the lifetime of its relationship with them.

Customized Presentation to Host application pattern

Used to provide a more user-friendly interface to existing host applications without changing the underlying application.

data mart

A data store defined and designed to meet the information needs of a group of users or a department. It contains the required data, either detailed or summarized, and structured according to the query or reporting needs of the user. Data marts are often used in a read-only fashion and come in a variety of forms, including relational databases, multi-dimensional databases, spreadsheets, and Web marts.

Data Mirroring application pattern

Enables integration of disparate applications by making a read-only copy of the data available to a partner application.

Decomposition application pattern

Extends the hub-and-spoke architecture provided by the Router application pattern. It decomposes a single, compound request from a client into several, simpler requests and intelligently routes them to multiple backend applications. Typically, the responses from these multiple backend applications are recomposed into a single response and sent back to the client.

Device Support service

Enables users of a wide range of devices to access the same set of applications

Direct Connection application pattern

Helps to structure a system design that allows a pair of applications to directly communicate with each other.

Directed Collaboration application pattern

Allows users to collaborate with others on the network interactively.

Directly Integrated Single Channel application pattern

Provides a structure for applications that need one or more point-to-point connections with back-end applications, but only need to focus on one delivery channel.

Distributed Component Object Model (DCOM)

A set of Microsoft concepts and program interfaces in which a client program object can request services from server program objects on other computers in a network.

Document Exchange application pattern

Helps to structure the batched electronic exchange of data using mutually agreed message formats.

e-business solutions

Use evolutionary technology and re-engineered business processes to develop revolutionary new applications that are not limited by time, space, organizational boundaries, or territorial borders.

EDI translation packages

Convert EDI messages from (and to) flat files, into a usable format for an enterprise's applications.

electronic commerce solutions

Allow enterprises to offer products and services to existing and new customers across new channels based on Internet technologies.

Electronic Data Interchange (EDI)

A standard format for exchanging business data. An EDI message contains a string of data elements, each of which represents a singular fact, such as a price, product model number, and so forth, separated by a delimiter. The entire string is called a data segment. One or more data segments framed by a header and trailer form an EDI transaction set.

e-Marketplaces

Trading exchanges that facilitate and promote buying, selling, and business communities among trading partners within certain industries.

Enterprise Resource Planning (ERP) Systems

Provide the major back-office applications of an enterprise (e.g., Accounting, HR, etc.).

Executive Information System (EIS)

Provides high-level business information (balanced scorecard figures, key indicators, and so on) to upper management or executives. This information is often delivered to the user as a discrete item of work either automatically or on-demand.

Exposed Application application pattern

Helps to structure a system design that allows specific applications to be directly accessed by partner systems across organizational boundaries.

Exposed Business Services application pattern

Structures a system design that exposes specific services that can be directly invoked by partner systems across organizational boundaries.

Extended Enterprise business pattern

Addresses the interactions and collaborations between business processes in separate enterprises.

Extensible Markup Language (XML)

A universal format for defining structured documents and data on the Web.

Extensible Stylesheet Language (XSL)

A language for creating style sheets. It describes how XML data is to be transformed and formatted before it is presented to a user or passed on to another system.

HTTPS

See Secure Hypertext Transfer Protocol.

iMode

The packet-based service for mobile phones offered by Japan's leader in wireless technology, NTT DoCoMo. Unlike most of the key players in the wireless arena, iMode eschews WAP and uses a simplified version of HTML, and it uses Compact Wireless Markup Language (CWML) instead of WML.

Information Access – Read-Only application pattern

Helps structure a system design that provides read-only access to aggregated information.

Information Aggregation business pattern

Can be observed in e-business solutions that allow users to access and manipulate data aggregated from multiple sources.

Integration patterns

Used within Business patterns to support more advanced functions and also used to make Composite business patterns feasible by allowing the integration of two or more Business patterns.

Internet Inter-ORB Protocol (IIOP)

An object-oriented programming protocol that makes it possible for distributed programs written in different programming languages to communicate over the Internet. IIOP is a critical part of a strategic industry standard, CORBA (Common Object Request Broker Architecture).

Java applet

A small Java program that is intended not to be run on its own, but rather to be embedded inside another application. It usually gets downloaded from the server and runs inside the browser.

JavaScript

An interpreted programming or script language. Interpreted languages generally take longer to process than compiled languages, but are very useful for shorter programs.

JSP

Provides a simple yet powerful mechanism for inserting dynamic content into Web pages. The JSP specification achieves this by defining a number of HTML-like tags that allow developers to insert server-side Java logic directly into HTML or XML pages that are sent to HTTP clients.

knowledge management

The identification and analysis of available and required knowledge assets and related processes.

Lightweight Directory Access Protocol (LDAP)

A software protocol for enabling anyone to locate organizations, individuals, and other resources (such as files and devices in a network), whether on the Internet or on a corporate intranet.

Managed Collaboration application pattern

Builds on the Directed Collaboration pattern by implementing workflow rules to manage the collaboration between users of the solution.

Managed Process application pattern

Provides support for long-running transactions (or conversations) that underpin many business processes.

Managed Public and Private Processes application pattern

Structures a system design that handles different business protocols with different business partners and maps long-running external transactions to internal business processes and workflow.

Managed Public Processes application pattern

Structures a system design that handles the management of shared business processes between business partners.

Message Oriented Middleware (MOM)

Provides program-to-program communications by message passing. It provides an infrastructure that supports reliable and scalable high-performance distributed application networks.

MQSeries

Provides heterogeneous any-to-any connectivity from desktop to mainframe.

MQSeries Integrator

Combines a one-to-many connectivity model, plus transformation, intelligent routing, and information flow modeling. It facilitates the development of new application services that integrate the functions of multiple, disparate existing business systems. More information can be found at http://www.ibm.com/software/ts/mqseries/integrator/

MQSeries Workflow

Business process management software from IBM. It facilitates the rapid development and management of the business processes that integrate the IT and organizational infrastructure of a company. More information can be found at http://www.ibm.com/software/ts/mqseries/workflow/.

Open Buying on the Internet (OBI)

A proposed standard for business-to-business purchasing on the Internet, aimed particularly at high-volume, low-cost-per-item transactions. More information can be found at http://www.openbuy.org

Operational Data Store (ODS)

A data store containing detailed, partially reconciled, and nearly current data used for immediate informational needs. Users can often write additional data to this form of data store. It is a hybrid between a data warehouse, which is accessed often on a read-only basis, and a transactional data store, which is accessed on a high-volume read-write basis.

Operational Data Store application pattern

Allows an application to access a consolidation of multiple data sources, where each source may be updated and controlled by a separate application.

operational systems

Are often transactional systems that implement a significant business process or task. They can be interactive, as in the case with applications that automate the Self-Service business pattern, or batch, such as legacy mainframe systems that run on a periodic basis.

pattern

A model for building and a design to copy.

Personalization service

Provides a number of approaches that allow users or the enterprise to shape the choice, style, and format of their selected applications.

Pervasive Device Access application pattern

Provides a structure for extending the reach of individual applications from browsers and fat clients to pervasive devices such as PDAs and mobile phones.

Point-to-Point application pattern

Allows users to directly address other users on the network using simple point-to-point synchronous communications, and then enables the users to begin a direct communication link.

Population – Crawling and Discovery application pattern

Provides a structure for applications that retrieve and parse documents, and then create an index of relevant documents that match the specified selection criteria.

Population – Multi-Step application pattern

Structures the population of a data-store with structured data that requires extensive reconciliation, transformation, and restructuring.

Population – Single-Step application pattern

Structures the population of a data-store with data that requires minimal transformation and restructuring.

Population – Summarization application pattern

Extends the capabilities provided by the Population – Crawling and Discovery application pattern by attaching summary information to index entries.

portal solution

Aggregates multiple information sources and applications to provide a single, seamless, personalized access for its users.

Presentation service

The foundation of a universal desktop for all the Web-based applications of an enterprise. It provides a common look and feel and language transparency across multiple applications.

Remote Method Invocation (RMI)

A protocol that enables a Java program to invoke methods on another Java program that can be located on a different computer.

requester interaction

Describes the style of requester interaction between one tier and another.

RossettaNet

An organization set up by leading IT companies to define and implement a common set of standards for e-business. RosettaNet is defining a common parts dictionary so that different companies can define the same product the same way. It is also defining up to 100 e-business transaction processes and standardizing them. Because RosettaNet is supported by all or most of the major companies in the IT industry, its standards are expected to be widely adopted. More information can be found at http://www.rosettanet.org

Router application pattern

Structures a system design that allows an application message to be passed, under the control of business rules, to another application.

Runtime patterns

Used to define the logical middleware structure that underpins the Application pattern.

Runtime Product mappings

Proven physical middleware designs to copy.

Secure Hypertext Transfer Protocol (HTTPS)

Developed by Netscape and built into its browser to encrypt and decrypt user page requests as well as the pages that are returned by the Web server. HTTPS is really just the use of the Secure Socket Layer (SSL) as a sublayer under the regular HTTP layer.

Security and Administration service

Helps to structure a system design that allows users to access multiple applications and information sources with a single security model and through a single security interaction.

Self-Service business pattern

Captures the essence of direct interactions between interested parties and a business.

server

A program that awaits and fulfills requests from client programs in the client/server model. A given application may function as a client with requests for services from programs, and also as a server of requests from other programs.

Simple Mail Transfer Protocol (SMTP)

Used for sending and receiving e-mails between servers.

Simple Object Access Protocol (SOAP)

Provides a way for a program running on one kind of operating system to communicate with a program on the same or another kind of operating system by using HTTP protocol and Extensible Markup Language (XML) as the mechanisms for information exchange.

Single Sign-On and Role-Based Access application pattern

Provides a structure for integrating several applications under a portal that provides single sign-on capability and role-based access to certain information and applications.

Stand-Alone Single-Channel application pattern

Provides a structure for applications that have no current need for integration with other systems and need only focus on one delivery channel.

Store and Retrieve application pattern

Allows users to collaborate with others on the network interactively whether the communicating partners are online simultaneously or not.

tier

A logical layer within a design that allows the subdivision of the application into major functional collections. Tiers can be further subdivided into functional components.

transcoding

Bridges data across multiple formats, markup languages, and devices. In addition, it adapts, reformats, and filters content to make it suitable for pervasive devices. Products such as WebSphere Transcoding Publisher implement this technology. More information can be found at http://www.ibm.com/software/Webservers/transcoding/

Value Added Network (VAN)

A networking service that leases communication lines to subscribers and provides extra capability such as security, error detection, guaranteed message delivery, and a message buffer.

virtual private network (VPN)

A private data network that makes use of the public telecommunication infrastructure. The idea of the VPN is to give companies the same capabilities as a leased private network at a much lower cost by using the shared public infrastructure. This is achieved by encrypting data before sending it through the public network, and decrypting it at the receiving end.

WebSphere Application Server

Provides an e-business application runtime environment based on open standards. More information can be found at http://www.ibm.com/software/webservers/appserv/

WebSphere Business Integrator

Enables you to seamlessly span the gap between your own enterprise computing systems and those of your customers, suppliers, business partners, and marketplaces simultaneously. More information can be found at http://www.ibm.com/software/webservers/btobintegrator/

WebSphere Everyplace Suite

A comprehensive, integrated software platform for extending the reach of e-business applications, enterprise data, and Internet content into the realm of pervasive computing. More information can be found at http://www.ibm.com/pvc/products/wes/

WebSphere Partner Agreement Manager

Enables multiple partners to participate in shared business processes that can be partially or fully integrated, depending on business needs. More information can be found at http://www.ibm.com/software/webservers/pam/

WebSphere Translation Server

A machine-translation offering that can help companies remove language as a barrier to global communication and e-commerce. More information can be found at http://www.ibm.com/software/speech/enterprise/ep_8.html

Wireless Application Protocol (WAP)

A specification for a communication protocol to standardize the way that wireless devices, such as cellular telephones and radio transceivers, can be used for Internet access.

Wireless Bitmap (WBMP)

A graphic format optimized for mobile computing devices. It is part of the WAP specification.

Wireless Markup Language (WML)

A language that allows the text portions of Web pages to be presented on cellular telephone and PDAs via wireless access. WML is part of the Wireless Application Protocol (WAP).

XML

See Extensible Markup Language.

XSL

See Extensible Stylesheet Language.

Bibliography

Alexander, C., et al. *A Pattern Language*. New York: Oxford University Press, 1977.

Buschmann, F., Meunier, R., Rohnert, H., Sommerlad, P., and M. Stal. *Pattern-Oriented Software Architecture, A System of Patterns*. New York: John Wiley & Sons, 1996.

Dan, A. and F. Parr. "An object implementation of network-centric business service applications (NCBAs)." Atlanta, GA: OOPSLA Business Object Workshop, September 1997.

Devlin, Barry. *Data Warehouse from Architecture to Implementation*. Reading, MA: Addison-Wesley, 1997.

Gamma, E., Helm, R., Johnson, R., and J. Vlissides. *Design Patterns: Elements of Reusable Object-Oriented Software*. Reading, MA: Addison-Wesley, 1995.

Haeckel, Stephan H. and Adrian J. Slywotzky. *Adaptive Enterprise: Creating and Leading Sense-and-Respond Organizations*. Boston, MA: Harvard Business School Press, 1999.

Marland, Leo. "Pervasive Computing and the Patterns for e-business." FTP site: ftp://www.software.ibm.com/software/developer/patterns/pervasive-computing.pdf

Porter, Michael. *Competitive Strategy*. New York: Free Press, 1980.

Index

Note: boldface numbers indicate illustrations, italic t indicates a table.

Note: boldface numbers indicate illustrations, italic t indicates a table.

N

Note: boldface numbers indicate illustrations, italic t indicates a table.

X

Y